Teaching Literature 11–18

Related titles:

Gabrielle Cliff Hodges *et al.*: *Tales, Tellers and Texts*
Cedric Cullingford: *Children's Literature and its Effects*
Andrew Goodwyn (ed.): *Literacy and Media Texts in Secondary English*
Andrew Goodwyn (ed.): *English in the Digital Age*
Louise Poulson: *The English Curriculum in Schools*
Helen Nicholson (ed.): *Teaching Drama 11–18*
Morag Styles: *From the Garden to the Street*

Teaching Literature 11–18

Edited by
Martin Blocksidge

Continuum
London and New York

Continuum

Wellington House
125 Strand
London WC2R 0BB

370 Lexington Avenue
New York
NY 10017-6503

First published 2000

British Library Cataloguing-in-Publication Data
A catalogue record for this book is available from the British Library.

ISBN 0-8264-4794-5 (hardback)
    0-8264-4818-6 (paperback)

Typeset by Paston Prepress Ltd, Beccles, Suffolk
Printed and bound in Great Britain by Biddles Ltd, Guildford and King's Lynn

Contents

Introduction

This book offers reflections by a number of English teachers about their work. Each chapter has a specific focus in that it concentrates on a particular text or author, or on a small group of texts. Not quite all the texts are 'canonical' in the traditional sense of the word, but, by definition, they are texts which are taught in our classrooms.

In the study of literature, the relationship between the text and the student is crucial, and one that has been most frequently examined in recent published work. This book seeks to explore the relationship between the text and the teacher. The student–text relationship is acknowledged in various places and must inevitably be relevant to the book's project, but this is not a *how to* book. It does not offer a series of lesson plans or a digest of ingenious new approaches. These are things which often transfer badly when one teacher makes them available for another to try. The focus of this book is a different one: it attempts to answer the question *Which texts do we teach and why?* It seeks not simply to list those texts which 'always go down well' in the classroom, but to illustrate the intellectual, cultural and emotional assumptions which a number of teachers bring to their work. In turn the book may well invite other teachers of literature to examine their own assumptions, just as it might encourage them to investigate for themselves, and thus for their pupils, some of the texts which the contributors discuss.

I hope another function of this book will be to show that the state of literature and literature teaching in our schools is a healthy one, for there are many reasons why this might not be so. More than one of the contributors draw attention to the conflicting demands of a prescriptive curriculum on the one hand, and the claims of personal enthusiasm and conviction on the other. As all who are involved in teaching it know, literature in schools has been a site of battle between conflicting interests for the past decade or more. All English teachers bear some of the scars of this battle and this book is, among other things, a testimony to the resilience of the profession. With a government-imposed canon of acceptable texts and authors, and an excess of testing at all levels, there has been every encouragement for genuinely thoughtful literature teaching to quietly expire. Compulsory Shakespeare at Key Stage 3 and a narrow and repetitive syllabus at Key Stage 4 do not automatically stimulate good teaching. The pattern of examining now encountered at GCSE is a direct throwback to the earlier years of O level and a methodology which many believed had suffered death by disgrace throughout the 1970s and 1980s. As a result of the most recent changes it is now possible for pupils to be less well read, less knowledgeable and less open-minded about literature than they once were. It is clear that the intelligence and resource of the teachers who have contributed to this volume is doing a great deal to counteract the intellectual numbness that the National Curriculum in English in its most fundamental form seemed bound to create.

This book is about the teaching of literature throughout the secondary age range, and most of the contributors themselves teach that entire range. Hence some sense of continuity might be supposed: indeed the organization of the book, with chapters on the teaching of each genre at each level, seems to support the perception that literature teaching in secondary schools offers a traditional *gradus ad parnassum* model. But this is not the reality: there are currently some faultlines in the teaching of literature, and this book is happy to acknowledge them. While there is a clear and well-policed highway from Key Stage 3 to Key Stage 4, once we pass beyond GCSE the road becomes a less predictable one. Our present GCSE syllabuses in English literature are not the best preparation for A-level study, and there is a great deal less reason than there once was to see A-level English literature as a preparation for a university course in the subject. Two of the chapters dealing with the teaching of A level suggest that various kinds of break with previous literary thinking need to be made by pupils, and one in particular suggests ways of looking at a text with which they will be completely unfamiliar, but which is much closer to those which are now expected in higher education. Robert Eaglestone's final chapter talks about the problems which now surround the transition from A level to degree work. It seems likely that the A-level syllabuses which are to be taught from 2000 may well go some way towards bridging the gap, but the gap is now a significant one and is of relevance to the work of those responsible for introducing pupils to texts at any level.

Hence the book's aims: to reflect the work of thoughtful and experienced practitioners; to show that good literature teaching is alive and well, and that literature can remain an important part of the educational experience of all our pupils, whatever the rival claims of contemporary cultures or educational legislation.

Martin Blocksidge
September 1999

Notes on Contributors

Martin Blocksidge is Director of Studies at St Dunstan's College, South London, and before that was a head of English for ten years. He is Chairman of The English Association. Having been inspired to study literature at university as a result of discovering poetry as a teenager he has always been keen to include poetry in his teaching, especially at A level. He is the author of *The Sacred Weapon: An Introduction to Pope's Satire* as well as articles on nineteenth-century poetry and Shakespeare.

Noel Cassidy teaches English and theatre studies at St Albans School. He is a senior examiner and coursework moderator for English literature A level, and has appeared in, directed and produced plays on the Edinburgh and London fringes, at arts festivals, in schools, on small-scale tours and in St Albans Abbey. He regularly runs residential creative arts workshops for sixth-formers. He has written several plays, and a production of his adaptation of Marlowe's *Dr Faustus* won the Theatre Clwyd Community Festival of One Act Plays.

Robert Eaglestone is a lecturer in English at Royal Holloway, University of London, teaching literary theory and contemporary European philosophy. His publications include *Ethical Criticism: Reading after Levinas* (Edinburgh: Edinburgh Press, 1997) and *Doing English: A Guide for Literature Students* (London: Routledge, 1999). He is Series Editor of a new series from Routledge called 'Critical Thinkers'.

Sue Gregory has been Head of English at Gartree High School, Oadby for seven years. The school, on the outskirts of Leicester, is a Middle School taking students from Year 6 to Year 9. The surrounding area is part suburban, part rural, but a significant proportion of the children come from council estates outside the formal catchment zone. The English Department teaches mixed ability classes and believes that drama is central to the English curriculum. Susan Gregory is the author of four books of teenage fiction, including the short story collections *Kill-a-Louse Week* and *Martini-on-the-Rocks*. She has also had adult short stories broadcast on BBC Radio 4 and written articles about her teaching experience, particularly the teaching of poetry.

John Haddon teaches English at Littleover Community School in Derby. He was a head of English for seventeen years and has also worked as an advisory teacher. He is a member of the Secondary Committee of the English Association and has contributed articles and reviews to *The Use of English*.

James Hansford was Head of English at the Royal Grammar School, Guildford and an Associate Lecturer at the University of Surrey. Teaching interests included modern literature and theoretical approaches to literature at A level. He was the author of essays on Beckett, Conrad, modern British fiction and contemporary drama.

Martin Hayden teaches English, theatre studies and media studies at Sudbury Upper School in Suffolk, having been a head of English there and elsewhere from 1979 to 1999. He has recently become part-time in order to do some writing and study. He has contributed many articles and reviews to *The Use of English*, and two of the articles were reprinted in *My Native English* (Brynmill, 1988). He is keenly interested in drama from the Greeks onward, and particularly in the theory and practice of poetic drama.

Clare Middleton is Head of English at Wheatley Park School in Oxfordshire. She is a Schools Consultant for *The English Review* and has published several articles. She has worked in comprehensive schools throughout her teaching career and is particularly interested in and enthusiastic about teaching literature to less able students.

John Richardson was a Head of Drama in Inner London and a Head of English at a very large comprehensive community college in East Sussex, before moving to Devon to teach. He was for some time Tutor in English Curriculum PGCE Studies at the University of Sussex and is co-author, with Peter Abbs, of *The Forms of Narrative* and *The Forms of Poetry*, both published by Cambridge University Press. He is especially keen to see the sustained development of creative writing, including poetry, within the English curriculum of the nation's schools.

Vanessa Vasey took a degree in English at Westfield College, University of London, followed by teacher training at Goldsmiths' College and an advanced diploma at The Central School of Speech and Drama. She spent the next seventeen years teaching in London comprehensive schools, first teaching English, then in curriculum development with the Development Programme for Race Equality, and finally working with refugees in language support. She is currently teaching English at Dover Grammar School for Girls. As she embarks upon her silver jubilee year, she is still pondering the relationship between academic success and human happiness, and whether the apostrophe has a future.

Dedication

Very sadly, James Hansford, the author of Chapter 7, died while this book was in the final stages of preparation. He will long be remembered by those who knew him as will his work as an inspiring teacher and a fine and original scholar.

Part I

Teaching Literature 11–14

Chapter 1

Choosing the Class Reader in Key Stage 3

John Haddon

Much can rightly be said against the class reader. It takes up a lot of time; it can allow the English teacher to settle into somewhat automatic modes of working; it is sometimes used for work that is only tangentially related to the book as literature; it can discourage variety of response and work; it can become very boring, especially for pupils who do not habitually read at class pace. None the less, the class reader remains a staple of much English teaching, and there is also a great deal that can be said for it – especially if we are aware of the dangers (and remember that 'shared reading' can encompass a variety of shorter texts as well as the class novel, and that it should be complemented by individual reading).

Reflection on the books we judge to have gone well in class can furnish us with a set of *considerations* – I prefer this word to 'criteria', as it suggests something more flexible, more open to reflection. Such considerations can be helpful in making future choices – they may help us to be articulate about what we are doing. They cannot, however, be applied merely externally, or replace the task of responsive, critical reading by experienced teachers of a variety of texts old and new – something we should continue to keep up, whatever the odds against it. At the heart of shared reading should be a book found to be worth the trouble. We don't devise criteria and then go in search of a book.

This caveat in place, then, my first consideration is this: a class reader should have a 'public' theme, something capable and worthy of treatment at length in art and through discussion. This theme should be within the grasp of the pupils, but not something they comfortably know; 'relevance' can be too automatic a criterion, and the content should in some way go beyond the majority shared experiences of the readers. The book should not simply reflect current clichés but be able to prompt thought; it should permit a range of response and opinion.

The National Curriculum requires attention to works that extend pupils' moral, social and emotional understanding. Some distinctions are needed here. Our choice of books should involve a moral *concern*, but should not (I would argue) stem from a moral *programme*. It's not a matter of making a list of issues or virtues and then looking for books that illustrate them or that enable us to 'teach' them. Teaching literature is not the same as teaching PSE. At the heart of our reading together is a book found worth the trouble – and that will include a moral dimension. The theme shouldn't choose the book – as far as that goes, we should be avoiding the 'issue'.

If we reflect on the books we find worthwhile in class, we will probably find that their themes are rather general: friendship, death, responsibility, conscience, identity, difference . . . To a large extent they will be concerned with coming to terms with something, resolving – or learning to live without resolving – a dilemma, or with orientation, finding one's place, knowing how to go on, or of moving from one state of awareness to another (usually in beneficial directions, but not necessarily). Occasionally we will come across a book that deals with something more specific and unusual – Betsy Byars' excellent *The Eighteenth Emergency*, for instance, is concerned with *honour*.

Fiction can be, as D.W. Harding phrases it, 'a convention for enlarging the discussion we have with each other about what might befall' – and also for enlarging the discussion we have with ourselves; but we are dealing here with what is to be shared in the semi-public space of the classroom, in which undue distress or embarrassment should be avoided. I'm not thinking here of the simple matter of tact – of being sure that no recent deaths have taken place in pupils' families before embarking on Katherine Paterson's *A Bridge to Terabithia*, for instance. Some things are too close for the comfort (comfort, not complacency) of young teenagers. The sense of what these things are will vary from teacher to teacher, and rightly so. Personally, I feel that sexual issues belong more to the private reading than to the classroom, so, fine as I think Berlie Doherty's *Dear Nobody* is, my inclination is not to use it. Similarly, Zibby Oneal's excellent *The Language of Goldfish*, which deals with a young girl's reluctance to grow into womanhood, is perhaps not best suited to the mixed classroom. I may well draw the line wrongly; the point is that drawing the line is important. Some of the issues that could be too close for comfort can be dealt with on what Winifred Whitehead in *Different Faces: Growing up with Books on a Multicultural Society* calls 'neutral ground'. Issues of difference, for instance, might be approached not through stories of racism in inner-city comprehensives, but through a science fiction novel. But for some questions – the more intimate questions – it is hard to find this removed ground.

It is idle to pretend that our own beliefs won't have a bearing on what we value in the classroom, but if we are teaching literature we will avoid the simplistic and the doctrinaire. In general terms I'd put it this way: reading literature can (although there is no guarantee that it will) enlarge my sense of what it is to love my neighbour – by enlarging both my sense of who my neighbour might be and what forms that love might take.

We are not in it for the theme – this is only the first consideration to be considered, although it is an important one. If there is a book chiefly of value in that it flags up an issue, raises a question – say, *The Wave* by Morton Rhue – it can, if it is short, as *The Wave* is, be read by pupils over the weekend and discussed on Monday before moving into further treatment of the theme that leaves the book behind. But if we are teaching literature, we want to stay with the book.

The second consideration is a practical one: the class reader should have a strong forward-moving (although not necessarily simple) narrative suitable for serial reading.

The narrative thrust is important for most young readers, who like things to happen. The ability to be serialized is important because the book is necessarily delivered in lesson-sized chunks with gaps in between; that is, assuming the reading will largely be done in class so that the progress of the novel is genuinely shared. Not all books have a structure that lends itself to this. It needn't be assumed that the 'episodes' have to be of equal length (or that each must end with an obvious cliff-hanger: some books, such as Robert Swindells' *Brother in the Land*, are marred by rather overdoing this). However, for pupils who find concentration difficult to sustain, short books with short chapters, each being a clear advance in the plot and discussable as a unit, may well be preferable. What matters is clarity of structure. All but the last of the staves of *A Christmas Carol* are long, but each can be read in a one-hour session, and it's best to bite the bullet and do so (and with such a book the teacher's greater skill as a reader is essential). We may feel the need to bolster the reading with some such device as that suggested to me by a colleague: issuing the pupils with a list of the main events in each stave for them to check off and supply page references as they identify them (providing a useful summary guide for later work on the novel). We *may* – but I think it is cowardice: a failure to trust Dickens, the pupils, and ourselves as readers. (None the less, I did it.) The clear structure of the three ghosts, the three time periods, the progressive self-awareness is a frame that enables the following of the plot and the grasp of the matter. The final short stave comes in one sense as a relief for all, and a sense all round of having accomplished something.

Other suitable novels might be usefully structured in 'Books'; for instance, *The Friends* by Rosa Guy has sections charting the phases of the story and the developing self-awareness of the protagonist, Phyllisia. Other books may not have the divisions formally drawn but may be thoughtfully divided by us in relation to our purposes.

Another useful form for a class reader is that of Berlie Doherty's *Granny Was a Buffer Girl*, which consists of a series of short stories, each about members of successive generations of the family of Jess, a teenage girl about to leave home for the first time. What unifies the book is that the stories are told (although they are written largely in the third person) after a family gathering before Jess's departure, and that they cumulatively impinge on Jess's sense of who she is. The stories can be tackled individually before coming to a consideration of the book as a whole. (In passing: a pleasant follow-up to this book is to get the children to research three or four generations of their own family's narratives and write them up as short stories. Nicely produced, with illustrations such as old photographs, these make splendid gifts from the pupils to their families.)

Mention of Phyllisia and Jess brings me to the next consideration: the class reader should probably have a strongly defined protagonist – not necessarily a teenager, and not necessarily one with whom the class will simply and straightforwardly identify. It's not so much that the pupils should identify with the protagonist – whatever that means – as that they should come to recognize what the protagonist's situation is. Nor is it a matter of the 'empty' character, the unchanging hero who works through a series of events or puzzles (the mere adventure story can be left outside the classroom – unless it's *Treasure Island*, I suppose). In Key Stage 3 it may be best to read books with a protagonist who changes, or about whom more than one opinion can be held. Jess in *Granny Was a Buffer Girl* is not straightforwardly a sympathetic character, although she has (I think) our sympathy, and Phyllisia in *The Friends* is in many ways downright unpleasant – vain, manipulative and wilfully self-deceived.

However, there may be sound objections to a too exclusive focus on individuals, and other characters only as they relate to the individual. Some of our reading should probably focus on books involving groups of characters to whom equal prominence is given – for instance, Jan Needle's *A Game of Soldiers* (brief, serializable, on a serious theme: perceptions of war) – or those that deliberately pair main characters, giving them their own voices. And while it is on individuals that moral issues are focused – it is individuals who choose, move, act, come to know, err, or go with the tide (although perhaps the latter are only individuals in a qualified sense) – individuals do not exist outside contexts, and the nature of those contexts (and how they may be said to influence or even to construct the individual) is something not often foregrounded in the fiction that finds its way into our classrooms. *Granny Was a Buffer Girl* does this to some extent through its moving down the generations, as does, to a greater extent and more subtly, Alan Garner's *Stone Book Quartet*.

A further consideration in our search for suitable books might well be to explore this dimension. A book that I would recommend for individual reading in this respect is Iris Rosofsky's *Miriam*, in which culture as a milieu, setting parameters of experience and response, is explicitly present as a subject of the novel. Miriam is a young girl in a very orthodox Jewish home. Her younger brother, Moshe, is becoming deeply involved in his religious training. The book traces her relationship with him and with the family of her cousin Rosie, who does not follow the orthodox tradition. After Moshe's death and her estrangement from Rosie, Miriam has to decide how she is to be the woman that she is to be – in what relation to the tradition she must find herself. She knows she cannot simply reject it, as Rosie has done, and be rootless:

> ... she was linked to nothing – a 'free spirit' – free to be buffeted by the changing times ... Life without the Holy One, a single day without blessing His Name when I lay down to sleep and when I rose again to life, would be unthinkable. But I would have to find my own way. I didn't know how I would do this ...
> I wanted Moshe to give me the answer. But the silence was palpable.

I find this impressive. I don't, however, believe that the novel would work as a class reader, although I would gladly be proved wrong about that.

This passage from *Miriam* is clearly well written, if stylistically unremarkable: quietly emphatic, with its variation of long and short sentences, it controls its rhythm across the paragraphs. Quality of writing is an essential consideration in the choice of the class reader: there should be some distinction, however modest, in how the book is written. This may be a matter of style, of particular precision in the use of words, or of construction, or both. The book should be able to provide models for writing that the pupils might learn from, whether explicitly or otherwise. Some of these features might be foregrounded for discussion in class.

The National Curriculum requires attention to the variety of authors' language use in fiction – but we will scarcely draw up a programme of, say, four novels over three years to demonstrate 'a range of . . .'. (Nor, however, will we stick with books of too great similarity in their manner, any more than their matter.) The variety of techniques is not the issue; the issue is what is being done – achieved – in the writing. Any technique can be used to little purpose. The quality of writing – not a question of empty style, but of the realization of the matter – is what is important. The question of variety might better be tackled by a series of lessons working with extracts chosen especially for the purpose.

In *The Friends* the language is clearly adequate, for instance, to the gravity and horror of the moment in which Ramona, the mother of Phyllisia and her sister Ruby, finally reveals the nature of her illness by tearing down the upper part of her dress. The passage, sustained over two pages, ends:

> And she left us, Ruby and me, with the burden burning in our shifting eyes, of the memory of the scars that criss-crossed like roots where a breast had been. More painful because of the terrible contrast with the other breast, which was so firmly moulded into the unmarred satin of her skin that it had to be etched in both our minds as beauty's standard.

There are no concessions here to a simpler vocabulary ('burden', 'unmarred', 'etched') or a simpler understanding, either in the subject matter or in the language in which it is presented. The light but emphatic alliteration of 'burden burning', the precise suggestiveness of 'shifting', the verbless main clause of the second sentence are all evidence of the quality of writing here. Not that we would necessarily discuss these issues with the pupils, and certainly not at the point of a first reading, in which it is our job as teachers to read the passage as well as it has been written, to do justice to the expressive rhythm.

The paragraph quoted above is all the more forceful for its coming after Ramona's savage denunciation of beauty – hers and her daughters' (a momentary jolt there for Phyllisia, who thinks of herself as plain), *all* beauty – as 'a low trick put out by God self', and her assertion that what her daughters must learn is 'how life twists you so that we put worthless values in worthless things. Puts beauty before you to blind you to what beauty really is. Gives soul, then makes it sinful to have soul'. All this, and yet 'beauty's standard'. Whether we would discuss with our classes the many issues raised here is a matter of judgement, but it should be clear that no thesis is being pushed – Ramona is not a mouthpiece. This is what this particular woman is brought to saying in the pain of her situation. (These considerations are, incidentally, far more important than looking at the features of dialect speech in the novel. If we want to do dialect, we should work with a less powerful text – or come back to excerpts from this one at a much later stage and with an altered purpose.)

Some books will invite us to foreground, or foreground themselves, questions of the use of words. For instance, in Lois Lowly's *The Giver*, the community, which has in its past deliberately levelled differences and removed, by social and genetic engineering, historical memory and many of the qualities in life that we – as the novel artfully demonstrates – take for granted, sets great store by precision of language, teaching it to young children with the aid of a punishment wand for repeated inaccuracies such as the unfortunate confusion of 'snack' and 'smack' ('I want my smack.' He gets it.) Jonas, the novel's protagonist, has learned the lesson well. He thinks carefully about words, deciding that what he feels about the forthcoming ceremony, in which he will receive his assignment for adult life, is 'apprehensive', rather than 'frightened', 'eager' or 'excited'. It is this awareness of words that helps his perception later in the book that 'it was a new *depth* of feelings that he was experiencing'. He wonders about the adequacy of language to convey the qualitative differences that he is learning. In some scenes the distinctions enforced by the community seem trivial and petty, in others significant. Precision of language seems to be both empty pedantry and a matter of life. In one of the book's most painful scenes, Jonas, having discovered the possibility of love, asks his parents whether they love him. Their response is to laugh, and admonish him for his failure in precision of language. He could have asked, they say, whether they enjoy him, or 'do you take pride in my accomplishments?' rather than use 'a very generalised word, so meaningless that it's become almost obsolete'. Clearly there is an enormous amount to work on here, and it is entirely germane to an understanding of the novel.

At times, accuracies of language may be more occasional but still worth pausing on. In the last story in *Granny Was a Buffer Girl*, Jess's own story, she is rescued from her entanglement with a married man by Steve, who fires at her a series of silly 'What do you call . . .?' jokes until she is able both to cry and laugh, and in a sharp moment to ask herself (the effectiveness of the short paragraph can be pointed out here): 'What do you call a girl who's attached to a bird of prey?'

The National Curriculum also encourages attention to a range of narrative structures. Questions of construction may well be more readily apparent to pupils than matters of language. *The Friends*, although written conventionally as a first-person narrative, does in places depart markedly from that manner. After the death of her mother, Phyllisia moves in a 'trancelike state between dream and reality'. At the funeral,

Phyllisia begins to hear a voice (soon 'the Voice'), at first just repeating snatches of what Ramona had said to her. These snatches are worked into a counterpoint with the voices at the funeral – the Preacher, Calvin, gossiping and superficially caring friends of the family, in a combination of script and narrative, building up to a climax in which Phyllisia cries out for her discarded friend Edith. Pupils can consider why the author moved into that mode for that section. (The technique had been used in a less extreme form at an earlier point in the novel, where too much is being said for the distressed Phyllisia to handle.) After the funeral the deeper level of meaning surfaces in Phyllisia's dreams, which the class can study closely, after which, and after her recovery from the 'trance-like state' (which some pupils argue to be close to mental breakdown), the Voice continues to haunt her, and to engage her in close colloquy about her perceptions and valuations – no longer speaking in remembered words, but independently as Phyllisia's emerging conscience. These 'conversations' are presented in script form.

Phyllisia's struggle for awareness, her discovery of her self-deception, finally comes down to her own internal dialogue with herself, issuing in the single voice of her discovery, after which the Voice is no longer heard, and the novel returns to conventional narrative-and-dialogue. Here growth of awareness and expansion of style/change of narrative manner go hand-in-hand in a way that is well within the compass of many Year 9 pupils.

A much more complex use of inner dialogue can be found in Robert Cormier's *After the First Death* (a book more suitable for KS4 – not that there's time among all the requirements that have been wished upon us). Complex narrative structures appear in a number of Cormier's books, perhaps the most suitable for Year 9 being *I Am the Cheese*, in which the intertwining of three at first apparently unrelated threads – a first-person present-tense narrative with just a hint of obsessiveness, a clinical transcript of some interview and a third-person past-tense narrative about a boy called Adam build up to a genuinely horrifying climax. I find that this book divides classes; some pupils are fascinated by the puzzle the novel sets and enjoy teasing out the relations between the strands and the slow exposition of the novel's central situation, while others are simply baffled, irritated and bored. There is also the question of whether a book with the awful impact of this one is suitable for younger readers.

Multiple – usually dual – narratives are now quite common among novels for this age group. In the best cases, and the ones most suitable for the classroom, the double narrative is a genuine means of exploration. In *The Pigman* by Paul Zindel, the alternation of John's and Lorraine's narrative voices offers more than one way of looking at – of conceiving – what is narrated. Pupils can look at how the voices are established – the characteristics of the voices (not just of the characters) and their way of feeling, and how these develop as the story unfolds. At the end of the book it is worth discussing why the final chapter falls to John, how Lorraine would have narrated it and why Zindel didn't want her to, and how John's first chapter differs from his last. (Also, of course, why John is given the opening chapter; and perhaps whether the closing words of the novel are actually beyond John's range and the author is poking through.) A similar device can be found in Robert Swindells' *Daz 4 Zoe*, in which the obvious differences in the language of the two narrators are an essential part of the book's theme.

I don't think this device is always, as it can be in some books, a matter of simple, limp perspectivism, a relativistic protest against privileged viewpoints. A sensitive reading might decide that, while neither John nor Lorraine has the whole story, there is none the less a whole story to be had, and it is the novel that has it. But the absence of an obvious single viewpoint may appear more easily to admit our pupils' own thinking further. It might also be possible to raise with some children whether rendering up a story to multiple voices isn't sometimes a way of abdicating authorial responsibility. (I do find it interesting that in two of his most successful later novels Robert Cormier abandons the 'fractured' narrative for conventional narratives in the first and second person.) These kinds of narrative very readily allow us to show that there is more than one way of telling any given story, and therefore to reflect on what is gained – and lost – by telling it *this* way. All this of course also bears on our pupils' own writing.

A handful of further considerations: the class reader should be capable of fruitful interaction with a variety of other texts – not necessarily just other novels, but poems, plays, films, television programmes, comics. It is here that individual or supplementary class reading can be usefully introduced. Things being as they are, there is also the pragmatic question of the extent to which the book can further our work on other elements in National Curriculum English – what opportunities it affords for speaking and listening, language study, etc. The time involved should be commensurate with what is got out of it.

A limitation of these considerations – of treating them as criteria? – is that they can apply to or throw up a second- or third-rate book: for instance, *Welcome Home Jellybean* by Marlene Fanta Sheyer. This book, written in the first person by a teenage narrator, concerns the return home from an institution of a mentally retarded girl and the consequent pressures on the family. It is of an easily manageable length, written in short chapters, with a clear and suspenseful narrative line. It can easily be grasped, and it is on an important subject. However, it is very formulaic: many chapters end with a blatant 'hook' ('I didn't know it then, but I was going to be back very soon – and the next time was going to be worse') and certain phrases turn up again and again ('Oh good grey grief'). However, this can itself become a teaching point; pupils do begin to comment on these features, and they can be invited to list the elements that all the characters have in common before writing their own parody or imitation chapter. (I have reservations, though, about writing missing chapters. Sometimes a more productive exercise – and one that takes up far less time – is to ask why the writer didn't write them.) And, like a number of second- or third- (I'm not talking about fifth-) rate texts, it is easy to teach. So is it a suitable choice?

For some groups it may well be: I don't think it's possible to generalize here. But I do have a problem, which I can best approach by remembering (with gratitude) my English teacher, Miss Hibbs, who one day had us banging our desk lids up and down as we recited Vachel Lindsay's 'The Congo' ('*boom*lay *boom*lay, *boom*lay, *boom*!'). One argument says that this kind of thing helps develop a strong sense of basic rhythm as a background against which to become sensitive to more subtle variations of rhythm; another, that this coarsens the senses, deafening us to finer variations. Can the reading of formulaic fictions in some way pave the way for finer work? Or does it load the mind with clichés that prevent recognition of anything else? (Of course we mustn't forget the narrative models that prevail outside the classroom; we can't assume that what happens in our classrooms is the whole story.) I don't know the answer to this. One strand of my training tells me that the best is the enemy of the good, another that the highest cannot stand without the lowest, and how these dicta relate to one another I don't know.

Whatever the truth of this matter, there is one last, essential, consideration: if the books we choose to read with our classes don't continue to mean something to us personally – to challenge or move us, to make us think – we will become technicians, administrators of literature, at best bored and efficient. In writing above about language and structure in *The Friends*, I became increasingly aware that in that book and in others there is simply more than we will be able to cover – than we should try to cover – in any one teaching. If the books are exhausted for us after one or two teachings, then I believe we should move on to other books.

Among the books I have found to meet all these considerations and to go down well with a wide variety of pupils is *Tunes for Bears to Dance to* by Robert Cormier. It is written in the third person without any of Cormier's characteristic fracturing of narrative (although the time scheme is not entirely straightforward, it is a good deal simpler than, say, that of *The Eighteenth Emergency*). The chapters are short, clear-cut; the book is economical, finely paced and proportioned. In substance the story is a morality tale, but in a largely realistic setting. It concerns an 11-year-old boy, Henry Cassavant. His older brother, Eddie, a successful and popular sportsman, has been killed in a car accident, and his family, unable to cope with their grief, have moved from Frenchtown to Wickburg. Henry's mother works in a diner, but his father, afflicted by sadness, is unable to work and sits in their tenement, rarely speaking. Henry and his mother want to provide a monument – a bat and ball – for Eddie's grave, but are unable to afford it. While recovering from a broken leg, Henry makes the acquaintance of Mr Levine, a survivor of a concentration camp. In a craft centre he is building a detailed model of his home village that had been destroyed, together with his family, by the Nazis.

Henry works for a grocer, Mr Hairston, a cruel bigot who beats his wife and daughter and makes racist remarks about his customers behind their backs. He tells Henry that he will provide the monument for Eddie if Henry will destroy Mr Levine's model village; if Henry will not do it he will never work again, and – Mr Hairston claims this power – neither will his mother. At this point it's natural enough to break off from reading and discuss the pros and cons of destroying the village, the factors involved, and whether we think Henry will do it. This can lead to writing: a useful vehicle is a 'good angel/bad angel' script which enables pupils to explore the issues in depth – and sets them the moral and technical problem of how to end the dialogue.

Returning to the book, we read a passage in which Henry is smashing the village, and we think the question is resolved until we read: 'He paused to inspect the damage before lifting the hammer again and saw a figure coming out of the farmhouse. The figure was Mr Levine, his cap flying from his head, running frantically, looking up in horror as Henry raised the hammer.' This dream sequence usually provokes a strong response from pupils. After this false resolution, Mr Hairston brings the date for smashing the village forward, and Henry goes to the centre, at each step telling himself that he will only go so far. To his horror, everything proves easy, and he is standing above the village with the hammer in his hand. Poised to strike, he cannot act – and then a rat (his abhorrence of rats has been quietly established early on in the story) leaps on to the table, and he drops the hammer on to the model village.

> He swivelled away from the broken bench, unable to gaze at the horror of his accomplishment. He stalked towards the door on legs as stiff as wooden stilts. *I didn't want to do it.*
> But he had done it, after all.

'Accomplishment' here is finely ironic – part of the literal and meta-phorical poise of this passage (and perhaps offsetting one of the moments of less than sharp writing earlier in the chapter: 'Trapped this way, as if for eternity.' However, it could be argued that that is Henry's perception, and that the irony of 'accomplishment' is Cormier's). There is also the interesting question of whether Henry *has* 'done it', or in what sense he can be said to have done it, open to discussion with no clear-cut or obvious answer.

In his final confrontation with the grocer, Henry refuses to receive the rewards for smashing the village; the grocer is distressed, saying 'It's not complete unless you accept the rewards' and *pleads* with Henry. Henry realizes that what the grocer wanted was simply for him to do a bad thing ('*He didn't want me to be good any more*'). Having escaped Mr Hairston, Henry 'Shrank into the shadows, shivering, not from the rain but because he knew at last what Mr Hairston was.' Again, this (very near the end of the novel) might be a point for discussion: What does this mean? What is Mr Hairston? Allegorically, he is the Tempter – does Cormier reach beyond naturalism here, and is that a strength or weakness of the novel?

The family move back to Frenchtown, but not before a final meeting between Henry and Doris, Hairston's daughter:

> 'I know he's your father but he's . . .'
> 'What?' she asked. 'What is he?' Curiosity curling her words, as she leaned forward, as if she was about to learn for the first time who her father was.
> Henry avoided the word he wanted to use. How could he tell the girl that her father was an evil man? 'Your father's weak, Doris,' he said. 'And he's afraid.'

The pulling back there – when you ask what someone is you do not expect an adjective in reply – is notable; and the word 'weak' thought-provokingly unexpected. It can lead to a consideration of all the characters in the book, the sense in which they are strong and weak, the different meanings of 'weak' and 'strong'. Even low ability children have been able to write quite well on this theme.

On the last page of the novel Henry kneels and prays by Eddie's grave. He prays, as he has prayed nightly, for his parents and for Eddie's soul and for his friends.

> Then he did something he had never done before. He prayed for Mr Hairston. 'Forgive him,' he whispered.
> *Forgive me too.*

In this book in which a clause of The Lord's Prayer, 'Deliver us from evil' is so significant – it is one of the two epigraphs – Henry comes not only to the point of loving his neighbour, but close to loving his enemy, as he prays for him that despitefully used him. This may cause disbelief, or it may bring about wonder. It may provoke discussion. Some readers will dislike the novel, others like it, for this overtly Christian emphasis. But the very least that can be said is that it presents something as a moral possibility (albeit, the Christian would say, under grace) and that, potentially, is an enlargement. The book is in many ways almost overwhelmingly sad: indeed, sadness is one of its burdens. Some students say they don't like it because it is 'too sad', but by this they don't mean that it is no good – it's that they like to enjoy books, to feel better (in a non-moral sense) for having read them. But one of the functions of literature is, as in Kafka's famous saying about ice-picks and frozen seas, to bring distress, to take us out of our complacency. *Tunes for Bears to Dance to* has, on its small scale, this potential. So, in its similarly modest way, has Cormier's *Darcy*, a book about a young girl and her best friend, who dies. This novel, in some ways a companion piece to *Tunes*, but more suited to individual reading, balances its gentler sadness with a fuller sense of wonder. But then that book contains a (private) miracle.

Pupils always wonder about the title of *Tunes for Bears to Dance to* (it leads them to anticipate a children's story) but they don't usually notice the two epigraphs at the beginning; the second is the following quotation from Gustave Flaubert: 'Human language is like a cracked kettle on which we beat out tunes for bears to dance to, when all the time we are longing to move the stars to pity.' There's wonder in that too (including the more colloquial sense of wondering what it means).

After reading a book like *Tunes for Bears to Dance to* – even more after reading a book like *The Stone Book* – it may not be necessary to do anything. Some books can 'put the quiet' on us, as one of Garner's characters says, and the appropriate response isn't to do anything, least of all National Curriculum things, but to go home. (Those who see in wonder only the spell of ideology won't be happy with this, of course.) As well as giving enjoyment, helping us to pass the time, provoking individual thought and public discussion, and providing models for writing, literature can bring wonder, and it can cause (we may hope salutary) distress. Both are beyond our normal compass as teachers, and they certainly cannot enter into our *planning*, but they must be allowed for.

ACKNOWLEDGEMENT

Parts of this essay draw on two pieces published in *The Use of English*, 'Wider Reading: Zibby Oneal' (Summer 1991) and 'Shared Reading: Lois Lowry's *The Giver*' (Summer 1997). I am grateful to the Editor for permission to use the material in this chapter.

Chapter 2

Crooked Roads in Poetry, Drama and Art

Sue Gregory

I have always been struck by the link between the visual arts and poetry. I suppose the connection was made early on when I became fascinated by the illustrations in Edward Lear's *A Book of Lear*. When I call to mind the picture that made the greatest impact on me, I discover in my ancient, yellow Penguin copy that it is indeed the very first picture in the book – of an old man with a beard, dragged from his chair but resisting, arms flung back, tugged relentlessly forward by the momentum of the 'Two Owls and a Hen/Four Larks and a Wren' who 'Have all built their nests in my beard!' No one is taking the slightest interest in the frantic-looking man who has been literally taken over, though the hen is looking backwards in disdain.

A different example would be Titian's *The Flaying of Marsyas* – the depth and beauty of the colour, the startling quality of the blue, the intent yet strangely detached faces of the watching satyrs, the scissoring shapes across the painting. The story from Ovid is gruesome yet awesome, and has a peculiar kind of beauty too. Perhaps *The Flaying of Marsyas* is a picture commenting on art itself, suggesting that the ritual severance of a creature from its very skin is the price that sometimes has to be paid. This genuinely shocks. It is the work of art in front of which Dame Iris Murdoch chose to have her portrait painted.

I want children at Key Stage 3 to experience the power of art to astound us, and I find a parallel between *The Flaying of Marsyas* and 'The Rime of the Ancient Mariner'. That is why I choose to teach 'The Rime' – because it says something so moving about the cost of being human. That, and the fact that it is so odd – with its witch's oils and blackened tongues, its snaky sea creatures sloughing off silver light and that blessing 'unaware'. The children and I read it aloud together – not all of it, only the first two parts – with as much gusto as possible. It is tremendous to read aloud – this terrifying confession of guilt and obsession amid hallucinatory accounts of a ship like a shooting star veering from cracking ice to searing sun.

The children immediately want to do drama, in particular this time on the subject of the dice game between Death and Death's mate:

> Her lips were red, her looks were free,
> Her skin was white as leprosy.

'Ugh!' say the children with gleeful disgust, already psyched up by the Doré illustrations. I tell them the tale from Ingmar Bergman's *The Seventh Seal* where the Knight plays chess with the Devil for the lives of the villagers. I ask them to anticipate what the Knight would do if he could see that the Devil was winning.

> 'Cheat!' says one.
> 'But the Devil is good at chess', I say.
> 'Upset the board?'
> 'Precisely. But the Devil knows where all the pieces belong.'

I watch one of the improvisations that seems to generate spontaneously. I marvel again at the way that, if the starting text is good enough, children seem to offer up, time and time again, deep insight unself-consciously and without pretension.

'Snakes and Ladders' is the game chosen. Very appropriate. The mariner and an agitated wedding guest play a game to determine whether the arrested wedding will ever take place. Amid much ribald dialogue a very crazed mariner takes a tumble down a particularly sinuous snake. The wedding guest has won and the albatross is resurrected, becoming a kind of clownish Holy Ghost, blessing, rather scatologically, what could have been a very blighted wedding!

The children then wrote their own poems, and to my delight one girl chose to tell the story from the point of view of the bride. She is 12 years old. This is what she wrote:

The Wedding Story

(Based on 'The Rime of the Ancient Mariner')

> I feel excited. I feel ecstatic.
> I'm overwhelmed with joy,
> 'Cause today's the day, I'm pleased to say,
> I'm marrying such a great boy!

I'm dressed in satin, I'm dressed in silk
As white as white as snow,
And nothing will alter right there at the altar,
The way I'll love saying 'I do'!

And then I see a scruffy man,
Who looks like he'll cast a spell.
He stops bridegroom Lee, then one in three
For he has a story to tell.

His tale is about an old sea voyage,
Which is set upon a ship.
He shoots a bird – yes, it sounds absurd
And his conscience is playing a trick!

This bird is huge, this bird is wild,
Its name – an albatross.
His shipmates say he'll have to pay
For the bird was glorious.

The golden sun, it fills the skies
With a gentle breeze about.
'That albatross brings rain and frost',
They say, 'without a doubt'.

And then there comes a heavy drought
And hail and snow and rain.
'That bird – by gum! – he brought the sun!'
They then confirm again.

He talks for minutes which seem like hours
As all do gather around.
And as he talks away, my wedding day
Is crumbling to the ground.

Finally he chooses to leave
And slowly walks away.
But where was the glory in all of his story?
And was it worth spoiling my day?

Not all responses to the Romantic poets are so profound. Lately the children's attitude towards 'La Belle Dame Sans Merci' has tended towards the flippant!

La Belle's Diary (Tuesday)

Saw knight. Seduced knight. Abandoned knight. Paid rent on grott. Drank some honey dew.

La Belle's School Report

ENGLISH: At times La Belle shows promise in English lessons; at others her brain resembles a table leg! Why does she keep yawning?

Here is an extract from a song about La Belle – from a lengthy piece with accompanying dance!

> What are we going to do about Belle?
> What are we going to do about her?
> What are we going to do about Belle?
> She made all the men's lives hell!
>
> She wound men round her little finger.
> Her voice was like an opera singer.
> She did them wrong, yeah!
> She did them wrong, yeah!
> She did them, she did them
> She did them wrong, Yeah!

La Belle Dame Sans Merci (modern)

> O what's the matter, cool dude?
> Alone and chillin' out?
> The grass has withered from the footie pitch,
> And no girls sing.

The stimulus for children *writing* as opposed to studying poetry can sometimes be a painting. Not a poem about a painting but the painting itself. Recently I saw a stunning set of pictures by Jennifer Maskell-Packer based on the childhood of Edgar Allan Poe. Jennifer had, in her turn, taken her inspiration from a text – not a poem, but a short story by Angela Carter from *Black Venus* – 'The Cabinet of Edgar Allan Poe'. I sent Jennifer copies of the poems that the children wrote in front of her paintings and she was delighted that what had started as text had returned to text via the conduit of her art.

The very first picture I saw made me determined to bring children to the paintings and to see what they made of them. It showed a fearful Edgar Poe, aged 3, awaiting collection by his adopting parent, Mr John Allan. Edgar is dressed in a cream coat and hat. The hat is topped with a black ostrich feather, and attached to Edgar's head by black ribbons. The small Edgar is clutching in his nail-bitten fingers a black star, the black star of the slave states, as Angela Carter puts it. All this is set against a dark green background, and behind and to the side of Edgar are a suitcase, a raven, pink baby shoes, a pair of lacy gauntlets, some coiling red ribbons and the worn out, gold satin slippers of his actress mother.

The painting led to the following poem by a Year 8 boy:

The haunting white gloves
Which belonged to the witch who murdered nine men and a woman,
They were hid in the suitcase,
But the ghosts of the nine men and one woman
Haunt the witch and possess the gloves.
At night the souls of the nine men and one woman
Return to the old witch
And possess her soul and torment her.
The careful black bird watches the witch being tormented,
And a tear drops from the black bird's eye in sympathy.

But the black bird is not what it seems.
It was once a man who was extremely selfish,
And was cursed to be a sad black bird for ever.
The ballet shoes were once worn by a phantom.
The phantom was caught as he practised by himself,
And the phantom was never seen again.

While all this happens in my dream world
Which is just like real, smell, hear and feel pain,
I dare not go to sleep.
The only thing I feel safe with
Is my black powerful star and my black wellingtons
And my white ghost protector jacket.

Another painting showed the baby Edgar balanced on his mother's shoulders and holding out a black star on a string to whoever observes the picture. His mother is dressed for the stage and her bodice has slipped, so that her breasts are partially exposed. A raven balances on the finger of her left hand, its claws like so many black rings. The following is a poem inspired by this picture:

I am reaching for the light,
The spiky black star!
I am scared of the shadows,
Trying to grab me.
There's a black bird pecking at my mother's temple.
He's stealing my mother's ear-ring and my mother just lets him.
I'm falling off my mother's shoulders and trying to stop myself falling.
However, I have to put pressure on my mother's boob.
I feel all closed in with our shoes walking around us.
My mother and I both have stars. Mine symbolises the heart
Of my mother and when I touch it, I feel safe.
It reminds me of being breast fed.
I glance down at my mother to see that she hasn't forgotten me.

I balance myself from falling, and all is well.
I feel safe and comforted. I hold my black star as tight as I can.

A further picture, not in the Edgar Allan Poe series, seemed to particularly intrigue the children. It shows a bride carrying white lilies at an open doorway. She is half in the room, half out. The door is white with an old-fashioned latch. On the back of the inside of the door is a black box containing honeycomb. The bees are coming and going between the lilies and the comb, and the box has been unlocked by a key. The key has a label attached on which is painted a heart. Behind the woman and to her left is a black cupboard, again with a door that is partially open. A white glove is nudging its way out, reaching towards a white coronet of organza or starched linen. On the cupboard is a half-opened box containing a sleeping baby – or a doll – dressed like a bride.

The boys in particular seemed to be drawn to the quirkiness and the touch of the macabre in Jennifer Maskell-Packer's work. Several afternoons were spent visiting the exhibition and there was never any reluctance – especially on the part of the boys – to join the trip. It became a kind of cult activity. As our school is a High School or Middle School with students from 10 to 14 years old, there is a feeling that it is quite 'safe', even jovial, to go on a quest in pursuit of prose or poetry. There are no older students to poke fun, and our students seem to find it very natural to spill out in words if they feel they've found something worth experimenting with.

Clearly Jennifer Maskell-Packer has her own set of symbols and metaphors that she returns to again and again, just as a poet like Keats does. We had recently been studying 'La Belle Dame Sans Merci' with its symbolist 'lily on thy brow' and its rose that 'fast withereth'. The influence of Keats on the poetry and prose of one Year 8 boy as he wrote in front of *The Last Day of July* seems apparent. This is where I find children's alchemical processes quite wonderful. They bring their knowledge of the poetry that they have read to a painting, for example, link the two and make their own further coil in the chain:

THE LAST DAY OF JULY

ANOTHER MAN, ANOTHER BABY

The lady of beauty and doom,
For whom every man shall fall.
Once the marriage arranged,
His virginity will soon be lost.
Another child conceived,
Another man deceived.
Two days after the birth

And the day of the confirmation,
The child shall be put with the rest
In the black 'end of life' chest.
The baby's Dad, the unfortunate man,
Has been buried the day before,
In the garden where only lilies grow.

A number of my favourite poets are artists too. Blake is an obvious example. My mother used to quote her favourite lines, and I can't think of better lines to learn when young:

To see a World in a Grain of Sand
   And Heaven in a Wild Flower,
Hold Infinity in the palm of your hand
   And Eternity in an hour

After Year 9 SATS some three years back I was asked if I would begin to prepare students for the NEAB anthology for GCSE, and it was suggested that I might look at Blake. I decided to try 'London' and 'A Poison Tree'.

When we looked at 'London' we started by reading the passage from *The Water Babies* where Tom comes down the chimney, to bring home the point about the chimney-sweep's cry 'appalling' the blackening church. That any church literally blackened by the fires of smoky London should allow climbing boys up and down chimneys while the rich (including some of the clergy) lived in such luxury is made very clear in Charles Kingsley's novel, where even religious images are the sole preserve of the rich. Tom comes down Ela's chimney only to find a version of (be it material) Heaven – all white, cream and gold and apparently with an angel in its midst. Tom does not recognize the picture of a man nailed to a cross and thinks it is very odd, but he suddenly catches sight of himself in the mirror and does not recognize his own image any more than he recognizes that of Jesus. He stares and stares and then suddenly knows himself to be dirty, a filthy black imp with snaggle teeth and stand-up hair – he wants to scream and run at the sight of himself. I told the children stories of the climbing boys – how often they were the runt children of large families, sold to chimney-sweeps for sixpence, shoved up chimneys as young as 3 years old and often dead by the time they were 12. I told them how the boys climbed up flues only 23 cm square – we made the squares out of sugar paper and most of us could cover them with a foot.

I also told them how the chimney-sweep boys – and some girls – had their skin toughened by being rubbed with brine and the soles of their feet prodded and burnt to make them climb; how the flues were a warren where the soot might choke them at any moment and how at night they slept on their often soaking soot bags which affected their genitals with what was known as the 'sooty cancer'.

Meanwhile, a group of students had worked out their interpretation of 'London' through visual metaphor. They worked on a rectangular background of which the backing paper was white. In the centre they placed a scarlet circle in shiny paper from which protruded a long beam, an elongated, attenuated searchlight ending in a point. This, they explained, was an eye, casting its baleful glance across the city. It was also the red light district which 'Blights with death the Marriage hearse'. A shiny blue Thames meandered across the display, broader in some places, narrower in others, speckled with red (danger, blood) and green (potential for health and renewal). At the top right-hand corner was a church cut out of purple foil, steeple and main fabric intact but with hollow windows. This church was disintegrating at the base, the purple running and bleeding. There was also a castle, the walls running with blood. Yet for all its horrors the overall effect was most striking – simple, dramatic, impactful.

We then talked about what 'mind-forged manacles' might mean, and the students were delighted with Blake's views on education. 'I hold it wrong – it is the great sin.' They also liked the fact that his father encouraged him in this, a kind of eighteenth-century equivalent of 'We don't need no education: we don't need no thought control'.

We also spent time working out the meaning of the last verse, the students debating whose *was* 'the new born infant' – the harlot's or the lawful bride's? They were taken with the paradox of the marriage *hearse*. To make the point about the double standard of many husbands, any of whom could have infected their wives with VD, I showed the clip from Neil Jordan's film of *A Company of Wolves* where Little Red Riding Hood says she will tell her granny a story. It is not about a harlot exactly, but about a village girl to whom the master of the big house has done a wrong. She appears at the wedding, held in the most exquisitely decadent of marquees, and cracks the gilded mirrors with her look. All the gorging dowagers and those puppets of the rich, the hired musicians, and, of course, the smug bride and groom are turned into the beasts they really are, with hairy hooves in silken slippers, an indictment of the social system that is powerful, if more gimmicky than Blake's, whose poem 'London' pre-dated the pamphleteering that would at last lead to a trade union movement to champion the cause of the chimney-sweeps and against the conscription of soldiers. Blake is one of the best political propagandists and moral crusaders I know, but he makes his points through images that shine on in the mind and lines so deceptively simple that they never leave you.

Blake also seemed to anticipate twentieth-century psychotherapy in 'A Poison Tree'. This poem went down very well. I invited the students either to do drama based on the two approaches to anger – letting it rip or letting it fester – or to do a display. Most chose drama.

First, in pairs, they had a rip-roaring row which they resolved by voicing frankly what had so galled each about the other. Doubtless because I had read the poem first, the children achieved a resolution to their quarrel even if the timescale was protracted. It would definitely have been better to outline each approach to having a row first – either voicing their grievances or bottling them up – and then to ask the students how they had felt during each. *Then* I should have read the poem.

When the pairs had their row about allowing grievances to fester it was interesting to see what had led to each rival metaphorically lying 'dead beneath the tree', and it was all to do with achieving at school. Rows were to do with cheating in tests and passing someone else's work off as your own. The result was not death but public shaming. I thought how brilliantly Blake had anticipated modern marriage guidance: 'better out than in.' Blake speaks out strongly against the harbouring, the pent-up resentment, which results, according to marriage guidance counsellors, in a phenomenon known as 'flooding', where one drop more is one too many.

One group then produced their visual display of the Poison Tree – an apple tree covered in fruit bearing the most tempting of words – but it was the root system that contained the most interest. It was very convoluted – a tangle of purply-brown – and along each root snaked a message: envy, spite, greed, lust, pride, covetousness. The children had, probably quite unwittingly, come up with most of the Seven Deadly Sins.

When we were studying the Romantic poets, one of our Year 8 students – a girl – had read with her mother 'Isabella or The Pot of Basil'. She began a dramatization of it with her friends. This started simply, then grew, and with it grew characters and props – a very large plant pot and a fine green paper head. The girls playing Isabella and Lorenzo started their drama, one crouched low, the other, hand to brow, gazing upwards, each declaring their love for the other and wondering, sorrowingly, whether there was any possibility that it might be reciprocated. In the end Isabella decided that she had to find out one way or another. So with great resolution she went to Lorenzo's house and mimed a rapping on the door. From deep in the bowels of one of the 'blocks' in the drama studio came an answering knock, absolutely to time, a little miracle of synchrony. I still haven't worked out how it was achieved. This is testimony to the level of detail and co-operation that children bring to drama.

A narrator declared the growth of their passion and also the fact that unfortunately Isabella had two proud and brutal brothers. Although the girls did not choose to take up the option of exploring Keats's description of the brothers' exploitation, I was glad that the girl who had originally chosen to read the poem at home had come across the republican Keats's magnificent outpourings against the extremes of the capitalist system and that wonderfully oily couplet, so reminiscent of Pope, that voices what the brothers really wanted:

> When 'twas their plan to coax her by degrees
> To some high noble and his olive-trees.

The brothers plotted and murdered; they brought the news that Lorenzo had had to leave the country on business and Isabella grieved. She pined and withered. But at the stage in the poem where Lorenzo would normally tell Isabella in a vision that he had been slaughtered, the girls introduced a further character – a little old woman with glasses on the end of her nose, looking very like the knitting sheep in the railway carriage from *Alice Through the Looking Glass*. This wise crone could tell Isabella exactly where in the forest the body lay. She led her there, still knitting, and it was very moving as Isabella, who had brought real stones and berries to school, knelt at the foot of the corpse who was lying in a kind of wooden cage that is kept in the drama studio, and spoke, changing Keats's wording slightly:

> Lorenzo sweet,
> Red whortle berries droop above thy head,
> And a large flint stone weighs upon thy feet.

The words were so well incorporated into a script of such excellent dialogue and the calibre of our students so astonishing that I momentarily thought the girls had written this magnificent poetry! What I can bear witness to is how pure and sweet Keats's poetry sounded. This was the most poignant moment in the play.

What I would like to teach together with 'Isabella or The Pot of Basil' would be 'Pyramus and Thisbe' from Ted Hughes's *Tales from Ovid*. A stunning reading by Ted Hughes of some of his poems based on Ovid is available, his slow, round, gritty northern voice lingering lovingly over 'Echo and Narcissus': 'Ech-o! Ech-o!' 'Touch me! Touch me!' I'd like students to hear some of this tape and to think about what it means to translate poetry that is 2,000 years old – to consider Hughes's playfulness, for example, when he spoke of Cupid's love arrow as being tipped with a photon. 'Pyramus and Thisbe' in particular would be such a wonderful poem from which to explore adolescence. I am sure Year 7, 8 and 9 students would identify strongly with Thisbe – 'A girl who had suddenly bloomed in Babylon, the mud brick city', and Pyramus – 'a boy who brooded, bewildered by the moods of manhood'.

Hughes's tales are so incantatory and hypnotic that, as with the 'Song of Solomon', I think it would be very easy for students to tumble into his rhythms:

> Sometimes they slapped the wall, in frustration:
> 'How can a wall be so jealous?
> So deaf to us, so grudging with permission.
>
> If you can open this far for our voices
> Why not fall wide open, let us kiss,
> Let us join bodies as well as voices.'

I think this would go down very well. It would be good to hear the wall's opinion on all of this. I'd like to hear the voices of the different bricks, speaking out in Hughesian triplets. While some pupils play the wall, I'd like others to speak out in the voice of the mulberry tree – to demonstrate how Hughes varies his tone magnificently. Like Keats before him – very much in the idiom of 'To Autumn', in fact – Hughes can produce the most lusciously rounded sound:

> At this time of the year the tree was loaded
> With its milk white fruit, that a cool spring
> Made especially plump and succulent.

This work would be especially good with Year 7 children, I think, as they have few inhibitions – children could each be an individual fruit tree, describing their wares in suitably fruity sounds.

It would be a fine text to help children away from clichéd simile:

> now they helped her
> Slip from the tree like the shadow of a night bird
> Leaving the house-eaves.

I like the way this simile says not only what Thisbe's 'slipping away' was like but it makes the parallel with what the bird is also doing. Ted Hughes's work as the building blocks for extended simile and for encouraging pure dazzle, both in sound and sense, cannot be bettered.

I am extremely fond of the poetry of Sylvia Plath, particularly her exuberantly riddling poems written during and after her pregnancy: 'You're', 'Poem for a Nursery' and 'Metaphors'. I wanted to introduce the idea of metaphors to a Year 7 class, so we started with the 'Metaphors' poem. Once the children had worked out what the poem was about (which they did very rapidly) they began to speculate about each line, laughing at 'I'm a melon strolling on two tendrils' and giggling even more when I told them that Sylvia Plath had described the birth of a baby as 'like a melon coming out of a key-hole'. The line that seemed most open to wild interpretation was 'O red fruit, ivory, fine timbers'. The group I had been listening to were just about to put forward their outrageous ideas on what this might mean when the bell went and there was the most massive groan. At the end of a poetry lesson!

The next week we moved on to 'You're'. The children worked in groups, in the classroom, in the drama studio, in the Deputy Head's office and in her outer office, lying sprawled on the floor with sugar paper and pens trying to work out what the poem might mean by *drawing* 'You're' – 'an astronaut', 'water', 'the sun', 'a tadpole'. I particularly liked the tadpole idea, as a tadpole is remarkably like a developing foetus. One of the children worked out what Sylvia Plath had in mind by calculating how many months there were from The Fourth of July to All Fools Day. I listened to the group's eager and ingenious exposition on why it was *water,* for example – the group jabbing vigorously at cartoons that looked like native Australian drawings to make their point. As I smiled at 'Well, we don't *quite* know why that is water but *never mind*', I experienced the wonderful recognition that every teacher rejoices at – that of *course* 'You're' is a tadpole if it fits – and that the poem is, well, almost about water. Poetry says it obliquely – it says it sideways on – and this is what the children were demonstrating: that whatever the poet may *originally* have had in mind, the images yield up myriad possible interpretations, so that the poem is a new poem, a fresh poem every time it is read.

The children then had a go at their own 'You're' poems. This one is about frog-spawn:

You're

Like a tapioca pudding made by a well bred chef
You are a dotted 'i', acting as the pupil,
Like a blackcurrant seed that will live to thrive
Snug in a rich soil
Now you are confined but soon
You will become active, alive, astir
To take a peek of the outside world.
As you grow you change.

You become more than before
And when you are full the time will be right
To start another circle.

Another favourite Sylvia Plath poem is 'The Applicant'. The black humour of the salesman's advertising of a 'wifey' appeals to the children because of its snappy, conversational tone. I asked them to 'sell' anyone they liked, giving their pitch as much edge as they could. The sophistication of what Key Stage 3 children can come up with astonished me:

The Ideal Pupil

Would it be . . .
The head with inside it a giant's brain,
The perfect one in society,
The one who is not vain,
Who does not cheer a fight,
Or switch off the light,
So the teacher cannot see?

Or would it be . . .
The one with the prettiest dress,
Whose parents are ever so rich,
Even though her head contains less,
And she speaks before she thinks?

Or maybe . . .
It would be a he,
Who doesn't play football at break,
Instead he follows behind you,
And carries your cake?

Or could it be . . .
The quietest one in the class,
Though still quick, one of the best,
When compared to the rest.
Whose heads are bare,
For they do not care,
They just stare, stare, stare . . .

Writing like this is its own justification. What I am hoping for, for students, when we look at poems or paintings together is, first, that they should feel at least intrigued and preferably awestruck at what poetry – and painting or any other form of visual art – has to offer. I hope too that they will carry with them into adulthood a sense that there is terrific excitement to be found in literature and art. It only takes a few good poems – a few imaginative pictures – to give children a view of themselves as discerning, discriminating beings in their search for what to read, what to look at. Second, secure in their powers to be alert to what awes, entices, excites and inspires, I wish them to recognize their *own* capacity to produce such art – as indeed they prove themselves capable, over and over again. Some of the best writing I have read in recent years has come from children. I want them to glory in their capacity and one another's. For it is when children go into free fall from poetry or picture, swiftly taking off and flying far away from what school may have provided by way of stimulus, that I am in accord with Blake:

> Improvement makes strait roads; but the crooked roads without
> Improvement are roads of Genius.

ACKNOWLEDGEMENTS

My thanks to Rachel Dobson, David Ling, Sarah Brownsword, Michal Heggs, Gemma Smeaton, Jacqueline Tedd, Alice Treherne, Thomas Feehally, Amer Haneef, Stacey Loughran, Lydia Gill and Anna Dyson for their poems, ideas and song.

Chapter 3

The Woman in Black and Maria Marten

Noel Cassidy

Drama offers pupils a rich palette; there are the familiar concerns of language, imagery, plot and character, but several different ways in which these are communicated. Crucially, it is read aloud and acted out, which tends to draw enthusiastic responses from most pupils, and not only those with extrovert or thespian leanings. This of course has enormous benefits in giving those quieter pupils a forum and a context within which to try out their voices, first of all experimenting within role, then commenting on what they have read.

It is a truism to say that plays are written for performance rather than reading, but one worth repeating. In the classroom context, performance can be interpreted in different ways. It is certainly unlikely that sets will be built and costumes donned, and, on the basic level, part-reading can be seen and valued as performance. The limitation with this is in stage directions, which can be an essential part of a play's means of communication, the extra devices after dialogue and characterization. To appreciate the particular methods of drama, an awareness of the theatre and its techniques is essential. One must be aware that many pupils' experience of the theatre is minimal, and some can see it as poor-quality low-budget film, since film is the medium that many are used to. Any kind of theatre visit, or visiting company to the school or staging of productions will help pupils realize the particular powers of the theatre and live performance.

Stephen Mallatratt's dramatization of Susan Hill's novel *The Woman in Black* (Samuel French; ISBN 0 573 04019 2) has proved an enormous critical and commercial success. The original London production started life at the Lyric Hammersmith at the beginning of 1989, and though there have been three changes of theatre, it shows no signs of diminishing popularity at the Fortune Theatre at the turn of the century.

It is an excellent play to use in the classroom to demonstrate the communicative power of theatre; it is very consciously a theatrical play. It is set in a theatre, guided through its action by a theatre director, employs recorded sound as its central stage device, and reaches its climax not by dialogue but by a *coup de théâtre*. These are all aspects of Mallatratt's invention; he departs some way from Hill's original novel to structure a drama which is, in a way, as much about the power of theatre as it is a version of Hill's narrative.

It begins in a Victorian theatre; a nervous man has hired the services of a theatre director to help him tell his tale, one which he feels impelled to relate in order to achieve peace. From unpromising beginnings the two of them re-enact the story, using sound effects to create a sense of location and mood, and the audience is transported into the eerie world of the ghost story until its terrifying climax. The reason why it is so successful at this level is that its staging is essentially very simple. As Mallatratt himself says in his introduction to the play, 'simple, straight-forward staging is the most effective'. As a demonstration of theatre, then, it is excellent. It does not depend on complicated stage machinery, laser displays or photographic tricks, nor does it drip with blood and gore. These may be the stock in trade of cinematic and televisual horror, but *The Woman in Black* takes place on a stage cluttered with the general paraphernalia of the theatre; it is, in the opening stage direction, '*unprepared for performance and devoid of scenery*'.

One of the first tasks I set students to do with the play is to produce an audience view of the stage and an overhead stage plan, drawing their information from the opening stage directions. While not a test of artistic skills, the task necessitates a very close reading of the directions and gives students a visual idea of the stage. In this way they are introduced to the ordinariness of the objects around the stage area, '*a clutter of cloths, boxes and furniture*', but also to the gauze which proves crucial in later stages of the play, and which divides the hidden upstage area from the downstage. Curiously, readers of the play have a greater sense of suspense here; we know that the upstage area will come into use, as we are told about furniture '*shrouded in cloths*' which is invisible to the theatre audience at this point in the play. The plan is not difficult, but does present a few puzzles to work out, like the position of the closed door which later becomes a dramatic focus. To increase the sense of theatrical reality, I have found it useful to give the pupils photocopies of real theatre plans, sometimes a scale plan of the school hall, but I have also found that local and even London theatres can be very helpful and provide designer's plans which can be adapted and photocopied. This work also introduces the students to some technical vocabulary of the theatre: proscenium, upstage, downstage, gauze, house lights, working lights. None of this is particularly advanced or specialized, but an acquisition of it aids an understanding of the play and can lead to discussion of particular vocabularies and of theatrical history. A quick research task in the library on the word 'proscenium' and its derivation leads immediately to the Greek Theatre of the fifth century BC and the beginning of theatre as we know it. The genre of theatre, with staging, devices and technical vocabulary, now acquires a historical dimension.

The question remains, to the central character of the play, and to young people reading the play in the classroom, accustomed in the main to the slickness of television, how two actors on a stage cluttered with rubbish can convey anything, let alone a horrifying ghost story. The answers are twofold. One is recorded sound effects, the other imagination, both of the performers and the audience. This realm of imaginative participation, of make-believe, is essential. Scenes, locations and characters are shifted and defined by moving around the boxes and furniture and wearing different coats; nothing more. In this way, the central character, the real Kipps, who needs to unburden himself, plays several different roles in the telling of his story. He is himself sceptical, as is demonstrated when the theatrical director sits atop a box (p. 12) to indicate a pony and trap, asking 'What could be clearer?' He 'surveys it dubiously' and replies 'It doesn't instantly say "trap" to me.' This simplicity, at first a challenge, is a boon for classroom activity, as the classroom lacks nothing which is required on stage. It provides an important theatrical lesson. As Kipps says earlier in the play (p. 3), it is 'expression and delivery, and ... confidence' which transform boxes or a classroom table into a pony and trap, or a solicitor's desk, or the desolate marshes around Crythin Gifford. There is therefore enormous scope for practical oral work here, to focus on that expression and delivery as pupils seek to create character and atmosphere for their classmates. There are other episodes in the play where this imaginative simplicity of staging is used to good effect, such as the long train journey which Kipps undertakes, where the isolation of Crythin Gifford is emphasized through several changes of train, effected by the actor shifting himself from one bank of seats to the opposite one several times, giving bodily indications of increasing cold as he moves further north. Another occasion is the rescue of the 'dog', Spider, from the invisible sucking mud around the house.

The nomenclature of the play is provocatively confusing at first. The cast list includes the Actor and Kipps. The Actor, however, is not an actor, but is the real Kipps whose story the play tells, while Kipps is the theatrical actor-manager who plays his part in the re-enactment. This carries more logic as the play progresses, as Kipps (as listed) takes the role of Kipps (character in story), and the Actor takes all the roles of those with whom Kipps comes into contact. The play remains punctuated, though, with dialogues between the real Kipps and the actor-manager, which on one level remind us of the theatrical artifice, but ultimately widen the scope of the story and present its true horror. The roles undertaken by the Actor vary widely: there is the ever-sniffing Tomes, the solicitor's clerk, and Bentley, the head of the law firm where Kipps is employed. On his travels, Kipps meets the friendly local landowner Sam Daily, who lends his dog Spider, as well as the inn landlord, the local agent Jerome and the almost-silent, seemingly imperturbable Keckwick, owner of the Brechtian horse and trap. As well as this, both performers clearly have their acting voice and their conversation voice when they speak to each other about the story and the theatre. Yet another tone is evident in the occasional passages of narration where the audience is addressed directly. Thus in a play which officially has two speaking parts (though there are also two voice-overs), there are, arguably, thirteen different voices in the drama. On the one hand, there is an opportunity here to experiment with the different voices, to get the pupils to recognize and effect the changes in tone between the acting of the story and the two performers' discussion of it. The audience can listen and comment on how successfully the tonal shifts have been suggested. A similar treatment can be given to those passages where enactment and narration are mixed, which is more subtle and more difficult to achieve. Pupils might consider the effectiveness of this combination, and the effect of having narrative within drama, particularly with the more descriptive passages, and this of course can be linked with the stage's absence of set. The narrative descriptions work the same way as they do in the novel, creating an imagined picture which here embellishes the sparse suggestions made on the stage. Ordinarily I find narration inherently undramatic, but here it works within the fabric of the play. It works theatrically, and fits seamlessly into the structure.

There is also great fun to be had in the creation of recognizably different voices for the many parts undertaken by the Actor. Each character is defined in the script, from Tomes's sniff to Keckwick's hunched reticence. Trials can be made by experimenting with regional accents and picking up clues about character types, which in turn can lead to consideration of stereotyping. Groups can try out their voices with different words to see whether other pupils can work out which character's voice is being used. If different groups end up with quite similar voices for the characters, as often happens, one can question what it is in the script which makes these suggestions and causes common agreement on something as potentially subjective as voice and accent. The extrovert pupils can run through their entire stock of *Woman in Black* character voices, but at the same time the number of roles within the play's limited cast list provides opportunities for giving a larger number of pupils a chance of participating. Less obvious than the different Actor roles, but useful to try, is having four actors playing Kipps and the Actor, two to play the 'performance' voices and two the 'discussion' voices, similar to the drama game where one person speaks the character's words while another vocalizes the thoughts. Pushing this further, one can reach the subtext of the play, and fill in the many pauses and gaps in dialogue where characters refuse to speak. Pupils can fill in those 'thought gaps', either vocally or in writing. There are a number of good opportunities for this kind of work in the play, such as Kipps's discussion with Jerome about the attention they seem to be receiving in the town square (pp. 18-20) or Sam Daily's concern for Kipps's progress (pp. 34-35). In both of these episodes, what the characters refuse to say communicates more powerfully to the audience than what they do say, and this is an important dramatic lesson for pupils. It is useful to look at the text closely to pick up the clues which suggest the unspoken thoughts. A range of techniques are demonstrated on page 19: Kipps's questions are unanswered by Jerome, clarified by the stage direction *'Jerome doesn't reply'* as well as his movements and responses which clearly avoid the subject Kipps is raising: *'(walking away)* It's only a short walk to the graveyard, Mr Kipps.' In the second suggested extract, pupils may well be surprised at how significant a simple 'Ah' can be, and will see how Kipps's own stage direction on page 35 demonstrates his unspoken thoughts: *'A long pause as Daily regards Kipps. Kipps shifts uneasily and glances away.'* In my experience, students at this level tend to make things explicit in their own writing, to tell their reader everything, and these sections from the play are useful examples of showing how a writer, here dramatically, can suggest ideas to a reader or audience by *not* saying them. It is not difficult for students to think of occasions when people avoid committing themselves in conversation, or deliberately avoid topics by shifting the subject, and interesting parallels can be illustrated through improvisation before going on to script writing. By looking at the whole of *The Woman in Black*, students will see that it isn't until the play is almost over that the characters speak completely openly, without this hidden level of unspoken dialogue. This in itself created interesting questions of denouement. It is necessary for the script to include a certain amount of explanation to clarify the many puzzles the action of the play has created, for Kipps and the audience. The drama has dropped in a number of clues as it has progressed, and Sam Daily's explanation of Mrs Drablow's history gives the audience the satisfaction of ticking off those clues that they have picked up and worked out. This is in itself an interesting test for young readers of the play, who usually want to create theories about the identity of the Woman in Black from the first few pages. If they can discipline their curiosity and write down what they think are the hints and clues as to her identity and history as they read through the play, they can check their version with Daily's at the end. It is rare for one to have worked it all out, so Sam Daily's explanation can be recognized as logical and appropriate, while being necessary, and this makes it satisfying. It also suggests that the play will have a rather cosy, comforting ending where all loose ends are tied up over a whisky and soda. Without spoiling the ending for anybody, pupils will soon see how this apparent comfort is important in lowering the audience's tension and expectation before the play's real ending, which in itself comes in two further stages, Mallatratt maintaining the surprise and twists until the very end. Here a great deal can be learned about dramatic structure, and indeed about narrative structure. Alert pupils will notice that the play's final surprise has in fact been led in from halfway through Act I. So much of the art of this play is in the careful laying down of clues and suggestions, while the main action has seemingly obfuscated the clarity of the narrative, and the audience is led through it by a close association with the main character, Kipps, who is seen both objectively, as a character, and more directly, as a first-person narrator.

This structure works to create suspense in *The Woman in Black*, and after suspense, shock. Back to Stephen Mallatratt's introductory note: 'The intent of the show is to frighten – so if it doesn't, it's nothing.' Suspense is not only created by these narrative and dramatic clues, however, and the shock is not contained in Sam Daily's explanation. This is where the simple staging comes back into play. I have already referred to the importance of this in firing the audience's imagination, and it is this enhanced imaginative participation which creates the shock. There are, though, no special effects as such, but theatrical effects. Many of these depend on sound, often in combination with lighting, but, like the dialogue, it is often that which is not explicit which creates the most effect. This is particularly the case with the Woman in Black herself, who makes her first entrance a little over halfway through Act I and makes about half a dozen further appearances, but she is a figure of mystery, cloaked and wearing '*a black bonnet that partly obscures her face*' (p. 20), not seen properly until her final appearance. Especially in performance, these fleeting glimpses are unnerving, but their nature can be picked up from the stage directions, for example, when she is '*momentarily glimpsed*' on page 41. As Mallatratt himself comments in his Adaptor's Note, 'something glimpsed in a corner is far more frightening than if it's fully observed.'

The self-consciously theatrical opening of the play, with discussion of performance and method, working lights and house lights on, and the clear introduction of the marvels of recorded sound, all have a function in the creation of the play's horror and suspense. As a precursor to Daily's apparently comfortable ending, it gives the drama an apparently comfortable opening. As the workers and the house lights fade, so the recorded sound becomes less a novel location-setter, a 'remarkable invention' which is 'extraordinarily true to life' (p. 8) and takes a more actively theatrical role. The first few sound cues do effect the transition of scene; we have the train journey, the hum of voices in the inn and the market noises of Crythin Gifford. These are important to establish the 'innocence' of the sound effects. It is only when we reach Mrs Drablow's funeral, which takes place on a bare stage, that the sound takes on a more unsettling role. The Priest's words (p. 20) are heard as a voice-over, accompanied by the '*echoing*' of the undertakers' feet. This is, of course, the moment of the Woman in Black's first appearance, and from this point on in the play, the sound plot is used more and more to create atmosphere and suspense. Even the sound of Keckwick's pony and trap comes to assume a far greater significance than when first heard. As it fades away, leaving Kipps isolated at the Drablow house, the sound cues work with the lighting and set to unnerve the audience. The upstage area behind the gauze is lit for the first time on page 26, revealing to the audience a new dimension to the stage, and a '*sudden, harsh cry from a bird startles*' the audience as much as it does Kipps. A short time later we have odd, sudden sounds punctuating the action, like slamming doors and the striking of a clock, but significantly, the next appearance of the Woman herself is in silence. This contrast is important; classes might consider why Mallatratt has eschewed weird sound effects here. The climax to the end of the first Act is all through sound and lighting. The lights gradually dim on page 29 until the stage is in '*virtual darkness*' before the sound of the pony and trap, which preceded Keckwick's charmingly rustic conveyance, returns in a powerfully haunting way, changing direction (by playing through different speakers) and volume before altering its nature altogether and becoming the sounds of '*draining, sucking, churning ... together with the shrill neighing and whinnying of a horse ... a shout, a terrified sobbing*' (p. 30). Kipps's screams bring a blackout. While seeing and hearing a performance of this makes the effect of this on an audience very clear, a surprising amount can be realized from reading the stage directions. A comparison with Susan Hill's novel provides explanation: many of the stage directions are accurate borrowings from the original narrative. It might be possible, with a serious group responding well to the play, to try to re-create some of the effects and enact the scene with them, but I must say that the approach does risk some unfortunate comedy. Pupils will recognize, though, the way that the response to the play is created by the combination of text with theatrical effects, and that these are therefore dramatic, rather than purely narrative, jolts. The pony and trap, which becomes a key feature of the narrative of the play, is first introduced to the audience in imaginative staging, then through sound effects, which in themselves progress from the representational to the horrifying, before it features fully in the spoken dialogue of the play. By this time, it has already assumed a powerful significance.

Sound, lighting and staging all contribute to what is perhaps the play's most startling moment in Act II. Again the effect is cumulative; the two primary sound effects, the '*rhythmic bump, bump, pause, bump, bump, pause*' and the '*child's cry*' (p. 40), combined with the pony and trap effect mentioned above, we have heard before. This time there is only the low filtering of dawn light, and Kipps needs to use a torch to give himself some illumination. The sounds, then, emerge from the darkness, while Kipps moves about the stage in his own small patch of feeble light. He approaches with trepidation the door which we noticed in the first stage directions, and which has remained resolutely locked throughout the play, but this time, in the low light, it slowly opens of its own accord, and passing through, Kipps reappears behind the gauze, revealing the room behind for the first time, and lighting a nursery rocking-chair frantically in motion. It is the events following this – the set plunged into darkness as Kipps drops his torch, the disappearance of the dog, and Kipps's near-suicidal attempt to rescue it from the sucking mud, watched over by the suddenly looming figure of the Woman in Black – which lead to Sam Daily's rescue and explanatory narrative. It is easy for pupils to recognize the way this dramatic climax works, with the gathering pace of events, the resolution of a number of the sound effects that have been encountered during the play, their combination with lighting (or more precisely, the lack of it – it's worth discussing the effect achieved by the absence of light rather than special lighting effects), and the final opening of the locked door. And of course it makes the shift to Sam Daily's narrative a relieving easing of tension before the play's final twist.

This is the moment when Mallatratt fully justifies the dramatization and the theatrical construction of the piece. He extends the story beyond its closing point in Hill's novel and continues its horror on to the stage and into the audience with a final twist of his theatrical knife. This is where the power of drama is most telling, and it is certainly worth making some comparison between the endings of novel and play.

At the heart of *The Woman in Black* is the story of a shamed unmarried mother, cast out by strict Victorian morality. I have found it very fruitful to examine this aspect of the play, on a plot level rather than a directly dramatic one. It is necessary to gain a full understanding of the central haunting figure of the play, a woman caught between her rejections from family and society because of her son and her deep, ultimately obsessive love for him. The discovery of her story is gradual, part of the cumulation of clues mentioned above. Some of the clearest clues, and the ones that give a sharp indication of her state of mind, are found in the three quotations from her letters which Kipps finds and reads (p. 39). These, along with Kipps's interpretation of them, can provide the basis for a discussion of Victorian family values and even current governmental attitudes to single mothers. After a discussion which places the quoted letters in the chronology of the young woman's life, a task set to write the full versions of the letters, incorporating the three lines quoted by Kipps, needs thought and sensitivity, but can produce excellent results.

Another play which has a similar situation at its core, but treats it in a very different way, is the Victorian melodrama *Maria Marten*, or *The Murder in the Red Barn*, available in a Heinemann Educational Edition (ISBN 0 435 23810 8). Here the conventions of theatre are enormously different from those in Mallatratt's play. The word 'melodrama' will be familiar to pupils, probably through the derogatory adjective 'melodramatic', without a real knowledge of what it means and its position in theatrical history. This can prompt a linguistic journey backwards from 'over the top' to 'a drama with music', the music giving key indicators of mood, tone and character to the audience.

Here the mother of the illegitimate child is treated much more sympathetically, as she is characterized very clearly as the victim of the villainous man, and though she too reappears as a ghost, her haunting is limited to her abuser, accompanying him to his final justice. Where in *The Woman in Black* the ghost is seen as an evil force, in the melodrama Maria's ghost is the agent of the 'all-seeing eye' of God.

This provokes a number of questions about Victorian morality, and with them, social questions. Most students will have a ready understanding of Victorian rectitude, particularly in matters of sexual behaviour. Yet in Maria Marten, we have a young woman who not only engages in a sexual relationship outside marriage, but bears an illegitimate child. She is, however, presented in the play as an unquestioned heroine, and bears some comparison with Hardy's Tess of the d'Urbervilles – she is similarly presented as a 'pure woman', separating the spiritual and the physical. Pupils should note the threefold method by which Maria's characterization as innocent heroine is maintained. First, as mentioned above, Maria is unquestionably a victim, and a guiltless one, demonstrated by her refusal to dance with Corder in Act I: 'Excuse me, Sir, but I never dance with strangers' (p. 4) and her reluctance to allow Corder 'to see [her] safely home' from the fair (p. 15). Second, she is a poor, attractive peasant girl who has no defences against the machinations of her rich landowning pursuer, who intimidates his victim with wealth and the glamour of London. Again, the similarities with Alec d'Urberville are evident and comparison with short extracts from Hardy's novel are beneficial. The final method is through the form of melodrama: the music. Music is so important in melodrama that it is worth considering attempts at co-operation with the Music Department when working on the play. When the audience first meet Maria, it is amid dance on an unnamed 'festive occasion' (p. 3). It seems to me that Harvest would be an appropriate choice, associating Maria with life, fruitfulness, joy and mirth. Later in the play she is accompanied by 'soft music' when pleading with her parents for forgiveness (p. 20), and music which 'turns soft and gentle' (p. 40), when she enters the fateful Red Barn. This contrasts, of course, with the music accompanying the villain William Corder, which is usually simply described as 'Villain's music' (for the first time on page 3), and varies in volume depending on the tone of the action. Particular melodies and instrumentation for the Villain's music and Maria's soft music are not suggested in the script, and it is certainly worthwhile trying to create some appropriate music. Many interesting effects can be created with modern electronic keyboards. The music is so essential for mood that some practical understanding could be considered essential. It is also good fun, and this is one of the keys to the success of this play with pupils – it is enormously enjoyable. Part of the source material can also be film, as we are now much more accustomed to this kind of incidental music in film than we are in theatre. Comparisons can be made, for example, between the Villain music and the ominous shark music in *Jaws*.

The varieties of ways in which music is used are interesting for pupils to observe and record. As well as the Maria and Villain music, there is 'Wild Gipsy music' (p. 6) for the introduction of the vengeful Ishmael, who seeks justice for Corder's earlier seduction of his own daughter. The music is often used to emphasize tone and support the dialogue, as when Ishmael's music 'grows quicker and louder to end of [his] speech' to Maria (p. 9), where he tells her fortune. In a similar way, Corder's music is described as 'loud' for his speech (p. 18) declaiming his intention to murder his and Maria's child. At other points the character music is used for the purposes of identification, often to create expectation and suspense. When Maria is left alone at the fair, having rejected Corder's advances in the first scene, the Villain's approach is first signalled by his music in 'faint strains' (p. 14). Later in the play the same effect is used to create suspense before banishing it, employing a dramatic bathos in Act II, Scene ii (p. 19). Maria opens the scene with a mournful soliloquy, which is interrupted by 'Villain's music, very soft and low'. She, and the audience, are immediately led to believe that it is Corder who then hammers on the door, but instead it is Anne and Tim, the bucolic comic duo. The bathos is even confirmed by their own musical accompaniment of 'Trombones'. Towards the end of the play, though, Maria's music is used to indicate her supernatural ghostly presence. In the scene after her death, at the beginning of Act IV (p. 42), her mother's speech wondering why she has never heard from her daughter is the cue for the music, which alone should surprise the audience at this point. The surprise goes further, however, with Maria's first ghostly appearance, where Dame Marten has a vision of her murder. At other points in the play, the descriptions of the music are not linked to character, such as the 'Tremolo Fiddles' which are heard at a number of key moments in the drama, including Maria's final appearance on William Corder's scaffold (p. 55).

On the one hand, the story of Maria Marten is presented very simply and diagrammatically: Maria's innocence and Corder's wickedness are established in the first two scenes: he seduces her, murders first their child and then Maria herself, but is brought to justice through the actions of his previous conquest's brother, and Maria's ghost. He is forgiven by Maria's father, which brings him to remorse before he is hanged. The moral lesson is uncomplicated. So despite challenging Victorian values, its moral clarity is still upheld; Maria remains morally innocent, duped by one with power: a rich, sophisticated, London-based 'gentleman'. As Maria says (p. 25), 'I am in your power and have no will of my own.' The play does play on the audience's emotions very obviously and directly, particularly noticeably in the use of soliloquies. Maria's innocent credulity about Corder's intentions are contrasted by the clear way he leads the audience through his genuine feelings: 'I await now my victim. Will she come? Oh, yes, a woman is fool enough to do anything for the man she loves' (p. 40). On this level, the plotting is so clear that it is useful for pupils to recognize the dramatic structure and the clear manipulation of the audience's responses. The sequence of scenes, the dialogue and the music are important elements, as are other theatrical effects, such as dimming lights (p. 4) and elemental sound effects (p. 41). We have already seen, however, that the use of music, on which melodrama depends, becomes quite sophisticated. Another sophistication is the dramatic structure: while the play follows the plan outlined above, the scenes are interspersed with comic interludes, centring around Anne and Tim.

The characters of Anne and Tim do provide a comic leavening of the tragedy of Maria and Corder, but their role is more complex than that. In a way similar to Shakespearean comic roles in tragedy, they provide a parallel with the main plot. They represent what Maria has lost through her liaison with Corder. They are humorous and simple, but their scenes revolve around their courtship. Crucially, they stay within their own kind, both being peasants, and they treat each other as equals, though laughing and joking. Neither has power over the other. Though Anne repeatedly dismisses Tim as a 'fule', he demonstrates witty skill in getting the better of a highwayman in Act II, Scene iii. The 'pull pudding, pull London' scene (Act III, Scene ii) comically shows Tim's simplicity in putting his stomach over his ambition, but it also demonstrates a character staying among his own and not being seduced by the city, where Maria is apparently destined to go. This scene develops more interestingly still. Maria, disguised as a man, as directed by Corder, while making her way to the Red Barn, provokes Tim's jealousy by pretending to kiss and flirt with Anne. Tim is offended and outraged, and although his masculinity is reduced when he ends up crying, he has demonstrated the depth of his love for Anne, which is again a contrast to Corder's 'love' for Maria. But this comic scene happens as Maria is *en route* to the Red Barn to be murdered. In case we miss the close connection between the two plots, Corder even borrows Tim's spade in the middle of the scene to dig Maria's grave, which he admits is an 'accurst design' (p. 36). This balancing of comic and tragic continues, with the penultimate scene of the play devoted to Anne and Tim's less than serious discussion of Corder's hanging, and even the last line of the play is given to Tim demanding payment of Corder's ninepence debt to him as the villain swings from the scaffold.

To a degree, the play can be treated as knockabout: the character types are clear and unsubtle. There is a direct uncomplicated morality illustrated by the play's action, and the role of music in melodrama can be explored. At the same time, there are lessons to be learned about characterization and dramatic structure, about the role of comedy and the expectations of audiences, Victorian and contemporary. *Maria Marten* is a highly enjoyable play to work on.

There is a good deal of textual interest in both *The Woman in Black* and *Maria Marten*, but both plays, in their different ways, offer students ways of recognizing the particular features of drama. In both plays, the live presentation to an audience is an essential feature of communication, which gives an in-built irony to reading and discussing them in the classroom. The tension and fear in *The Woman in Black*, and the balance between pity and humour in *Maria Marten*, are best appreciated in performance, which makes some attempt at dramatic presentation in the classroom extremely important, as well as being a useful contribution to pupils' speaking and listening skills. Both plays also offer insight into the other elements which make up drama: staging, lighting, sound and music. From the simple setting of *The Woman in Black* to the many different locations of *Maria Marten*, from the cumulative effect of repeated sounds to the atmospheric music composition of melodrama, there is much to discuss and much with which to experiment. Either of these two plays offers pupils at Key Stage 3 an introduction to the arts of drama at a sophisticated level, and would prepare them well for further study of the genre at GCSE.

Part II

Teaching Literature 14-16

Chapter 4

The Brontës and Me

Vanessa Vasey

I'll get on to the Brontës in a minute; let's start with *me*. On my wall at home is a sepia photograph of a serious girl with a pale face and a stiff silk gown. This 16- or 17-year-old in her flounced taffeta is my great-grandmother, Harriet Maria. With a bit of adding and subtracting and a few educated guesses, I have worked out that my Granny Brooker was just about the same age as Charlotte Brontë's unborn child might have been had things worked out differently. Thus do I reach out across the years to Charlotte, and find her closer than expected.

Pregnant in her late thirties, Charlotte seems to have wasted away from constant nausea. Her one-time hero, the great Thackeray of *Vanity Fair*, apparently thought tight-lacing had shortened her life: she had the smallest waist he had ever seen. That puts a new perspective on her heroine's 'piquant neatness' in *Shirley* (ch. 6): the constricted silhouette would, presumably, be neat – and decidedly *piquant* for the girl inside the corset!

Charlotte; what could she do? Stunted, and with terrible teeth, she wanted passionate fulfilment with a handsome young Dr John, just as did Lucy Snowe in *Villette*. But Charlotte and Lucy both knew that the hunky Dr Johns of life and fiction choose blonde airheads every time. Left alone with Dad, a crusty old gimmer and no company at all, Charlotte finally found a man to settle for. The Revd Arthur Bell Nicholls with his astounding beard, and brain on tramlines, was truly-madly-deeply in love; the full, sweaty, panting passionate affair that Charlotte had sought with one dud no-hoper after another. Finally it was on offer. Arthur wasn't cute, he wasn't clever, he wasn't even especially nice, but he wanted her in his arms and in his bed; that irresistible, undeniable, life-affirming animal desire.

And talking of unbridled lust – Charlotte and Emily knew all about it.

(And so did Anne; why leave her out? She wrote two good books, too.) Their heroines come face-to-face with it round every corner, and it's still giving us cause for concern in our modern, secular society. Free love and the swinging sixties didn't last. In this new millennium we seem far more concerned with family values than with individual freedom or the pursuit of pleasure. Which brings me to a favourite topic: the moral absolute. Students get wary and confused when confronted by Good and Evil. They try to dwindle evil away in a series of psychological explanations ('It all depends on the context') as if to understand is somehow to defuse, if not actually excuse, an act of moral turpitude – and surely we can understand once the historical, social or psychological explanation has been expounded.

It is as well to point out that all literature, indeed all art, originated in religious ritual and therefore served a spiritual and moral function. Classical tragedy invited the audience to fear the gods and pity their victims. We witness the irresistible forces of destiny operating on the protagonist, who, however innocent he may be as an individual, shares the guilt of his ancestors. The dramatic ritual of enactment draws us into his ordeal and we suffer with him, vicariously. At the end we are left purged through the action of catharsis, and, more significantly, at once humbled and reassured that 'the gods are just' (*King Lear*, Act V, Scene iii, l.170).

It is fun to discuss characters in plays or novels as if they were real people; indeed, it is one proof of artistic success if the author can make us believe in her creations. But the study of literature is rather different from the study of psychology or sociology or history; a novel is an artistic whole and needs to be considered as such. The characters and themes are there to convey meaning: they are elements in the structural whole which needs to be considered in its entirety if the author's intention is to be fully apprehended. In *Jane Eyre*, Charlotte presents an essentially ordered and moral world. Jane of the Gateshead and Lowood episodes wins through to eventual happiness, not in spite of her suffering but because of it: 'The more solitary, the more friendless, the more unsustained I am, the more I respect myself. I will keep the law given by God; sanctioned by man' (*Jane Eyre*, ch. 27). Charlotte puts her heroine under immense pressure to break those moral and social laws, and rewards her resistance. Charlotte and Jane know Evil when they see it, and their stalwart response is to tighten their moral corsets another notch.

For Charlotte, Emily and Anne, sexual desire must remain unfulfilled: Cathy, suffocating in her bedroom at the Grange, begging for the window to be opened to let in the moorland storm; Jane, fleeing from her bigamous lover, making her bed on the open moor: 'Beside the crag,

the heath was very deep: when I lay down my feet were buried in it'
(*Jane Eyre*, ch. 28).

These passages are emblematic of frustrated desire. Cathy and
Heathcliff unite only after death, when the urgent visceral nature of
their love has been purged into something finer and literally spiritual.
For Jane and Rochester, union comes after moral cleansing, and only
after the madwoman in the attic has been refined by fire. Jane Eyre
presses her lips and her knees together, adjusts her Quakerish dress (the
black or the charcoal grey today?) and pulls the corset in another notch.
Piquant neatness!

Jane is an elf, a bird, a fairy. You'd never get Bertha Mason into those
weeny little stays. The thing is, of course, that once the corset is
loosened, the purple, grunting madwoman will burst out like the genii
out of the bottle. Or is that another book?

The answer to that is yes, that is another book, and Jean Rhys wrote it:
Wide Sargasso Sea. She sets it in the same period as *Jane Eyre* but takes
as her theme the preoccupation of so many writers of the twentieth
century, alienation. Her heroine loses everything: home, family, fortune,
name, even her very identity. It is the unbearably sad story of Rochester
and the first Mrs Rochester, Charlotte Brontë's Bertha Mason, whom
Jean Rhys traces back to her earlier identity as Antoinette Cosway. Jean
Rhys invites us to understand, even pity, the cold-hearted Englishman
who crushes his lovely, passionate young wife just as he crushes the
frangipani wedding wreath under careless feet. Ultimately, Antoinette's
loss is not what Rochester takes from her but what she gives away. Hers
is the tragedy of the open hand and open heart. She gives her love
everything and is left empty. But Antoinette–Bertha retains life even
when sanity deserts her, and that spark of life eventually burns down the
prison, lights up the frozen moor and carries her home to the teeming
heart of the Caribbean.

Jean Rhys's heroine loses all on her journey from paradise to prison.
Charlotte sends her heroine on the opposite journey; from confinement
in the red-room to perfect happiness at Ferndean. Both heroines learn, in
an essential way, to transcend the binding power of men's love; a power
which threatens to degrade and dispossess them and to take away their
very identity, changing Jane Eyre into Jane Rochester and Antoinette
Cosway into Bertha Mason. Antoinette keeps back only the hot spark of
life itself. Jane tightens her moral corset. The message in both books is
that a woman is easy prey. Marriage on his terms spells disaster.
Antoinette gives fortune, freedom, body and soul, and Rochester takes
it all. The other Rochester would have pulled a similar stunt on Jane if
she had consented to an irregular union. Later, St John Rivers makes a
similar bid to control her, telling her it is God's will that she join him on

his mission to the Hindus as his wife. Jane will not: a triumphant assertion of her will. And Charlotte rewards her with fortune, family, a final hard-won independence, and, the crowning glory, a lover, tamed but still virile; redeemed but still passionate; a union in which Jane is an equal, if not superior, partner. Jane gets it all; and we don't grudge her one whit.

A-level students have produced inspired work comparing *Jane Eyre* and *Wide Sargasso Sea*. At Key Stage 4, however, I am more inclined to present a series of passages from *Wide Sargasso Sea*, for comparison with the full text of *Jane Eyre*. The honeymoon journey to Granbois, near the opening of Part 2, is an engrossing study of Rochester's sense of alienation:

> I understood why the porter had called it a wild place. Not only wild but menacing. Those hills would close in on you.
> 'What an extreme green,' was all I could say ... Everything is too much, too much purple, too much green. The flowers too red, the mountains too high, the hills too near. And the woman is a stranger ... I have sold my soul.
> (*Wide Sargasso Sea*, p. 58)

Charlotte's landscape may be wild and hostile, but her heroine is never tormented by Jean Rhys's paralysing alienation:

> I struck straight into the heath; I held on to a hollow I saw deeply furrowing the brown moorside; I watched kneedeep in its dark growth; I turned with its turnings, and finding a moss-blackened granite crag in a hidden angle, I sat down under it. High banks of moor were about me; the crag protected my head: the sky was over that.
> (*Jane Eyre*, ch. 28)

These exercises in comparison shed light on both novels and point up Charlotte's moral world. Jane meets suffering with ever-increasing understanding and fortitude: Antoinette's suffering brings disintegration and death. There we have the unflinching faith and determination of the nineteenth century and the terror and despair of the twentieth. It makes me think of Blake's *Songs of Innocence and Experience*. 'The Tyger' confounds us because we have seen 'The Lamb'. Jean Rhys's theme reflects her century's sense of loss and bewilderment as God becomes, no longer the Good Shepherd, but the master of the furnace and the anvil.

There are other interesting aspects of comparison between the novels: the use of the first-person narrative, for example. Jean Rhys struggled long and hard to find her way forward for the second half of her book. Then it came to her: the narrator must change; we must hear

Rochester's account at first hand. The effect of first- or second-person narrative style provides an interesting study at KS4. Younger writers (and older ones too) often slip between first and third person in their stories. Emily Brontë does this with consummate ease in *Wuthering Heights* with her complex narrative layers. Charlotte's contemporaries annoyed her by confusing author with heroine, no doubt influenced by the assertive 'I' of her story: 'And reader, do you think I feared [Mr Rochester] in his blind ferocity? – If you do, you little know me' (*Jane Eyre*, ch. 37).

Another point of comparison is both authors' use of symbol and thematic imagery: the poetic aspects of the novels. For example, an exercise to gather references to fire and water in both novels produces an interestingly long list. And fire and water are the elemental forces of purification: destruction and rebirth. (What was Rochester's mad wife called? How does she attack him in his bed in Chapter 20? How does Jane save him? And so it goes on.)

Jane Eyre is one of a number of nineteenth-century novels which seem, from our modern perspective, to propound a kind of feminism. On the leads of Thornfield, Jane bemoans the 'Millions ... condemned to a stiller doom than mine, and millions ... in silent revolt against their lot' (*Jane Eyre*, ch. 12).

No doubt the novel seemed bold and uncompromising, even scandalous in its day. In a way, the whole point of Jane's life, the whole point of life for the Brontë sisters themselves, is to achieve autonomy: specifically, financial independence. Girls and young women today find it hard to get their heads around the circumstances of their great-grandmothers (not so very long ago) who, if they had pretensions to middle-class gentility, had to choose between work and marriage. (The working-class woman had the delicious freedom to marry, bear children, and keep up a fulfilling career in heavy scrubbing for her social betters.) In Jane Eyre's day there was only one career open to the middle-class girl: teaching. Jane calls it 'servitude' (ch. 10). I couldn't possibly comment.

The Brontë sisters don't seem to have pursued the marriage option at all. They grasped the nettle of independence and set about educating themselves to become employable governesses or (was this better or worse?) school ma'ams. Look at the school ma'ams in the works of Charlotte Brontë: Miss Scatcherd the crazed sadist, and Miss Miller the worn out drudge in *Jane Eyre*. And the motley foreign crew of *Villette*. But, on the plus side, we have Mary and Diana Rivers. You notice that this erudite pair, first encountered bending diligently over their German studies (*Jane Eyre*, ch. 28), as no doubt the Brontës themselves might have done, are spared the hideous fate of becoming governesses:

Diana and Mary Rivers are both married . . . Diana's husband is a captain in the navy, a gallant officer, and a good man. Mary's is a clergyman, a college friend of her brother's, and, from his attainment and principles, worthy of the connexion.

(Jane Eyre, ch. 38)

Of course, it is Jane's inheritance which initially saves them from this slavery. By a delightful irony, when the Rivers family are cheated of their expected inheritance, they discover the money has gone to a new-found cousin. Jane finds modest fortune, and her dearest friends are revealed as her first natural relations (the Reeds having proved decidedly *un*natural). Jane has arrived; or, rather, she is very near her destination. The message is clear: 'a room of one's own' as Virginia Woolf pointed out, and a small, independent income. Result (*pace* Mr Micawber): happiness.

Women are supposed to be very calm generally: but women feel just as men feel; they need exercise for their faculties, and a field for their efforts as much as their brothers do; they suffer from too rigid a constraint, too absolute a stagnation, precisely as men would suffer; and it is narrow-minded in their more privileged fellow-creatures to say that they ought to confine themselves to making puddings and knitting stockings, to playing on the piano and embroidering bags. It is thoughtless to condemn them or laugh at them, if they seek to do more or learn more than custom has pronounced necessary for their sex.

(Jane Eyre, ch. 12)

All Charlotte Brontë's novels provide food for feminist thought, just as they provide tasty fare for those who like a romantic love-story. In *Jane Eyre* and *Villette* there is even a strong dash of Gothic horror, and there is social comment in all the novels, if not downright protest. Charlotte spreads her taffeta skirt over several genres; even the historical novel, in *Shirley*. But for me, the main interest lies in the moral meaning of the work, and in *Jane Eyre*, that means the allegorical aspects.

Look at *The Pilgrim's Progress* by John Bunyan for the structural model for *Jane Eyre*: life as a journey. Christian leaves the City of Destruction and travels from location to location, skirting hazards, finding friends, until he crosses the river and enters the Celestial City. Jane leaves Gateshead Hall and travels from location to location until she achieves Ferndean Manor and perfect happiness. There is even a wicket gate set before Moor House (*Jane Eyre*, ch. 28) and a light to guide her steps, just as Bunyan provides for his pilgrim. Clearly, *Jane Eyre* is not an allegory in the strict sense: it is, after all, a novel. But Charlotte has loaded place and character names with poetic resonance: the Reeds are morally weak and pliable, bending when they should hold firm. Jane Eyre will find the liberty for which she gasps as someone suffocating might gasp for air: 'I desired liberty; for liberty I gasped; for liberty I uttered a prayer; it seemed scattered on the wind then faintly blowing' (*Jane Eyre*, ch. 10).

Rochester is presented as strong, enduring in his way, craggily attractive as the rock his name suggests; and with a history as spicy and cynical as the eighteenth-century poet and notorious roué, John Wilmot, Earl of Rochester. St John Rivers is the aptly named missionary, off to baptize the heathen. Two virgins of religions ancient and modern supply the names for the kind and scholarly Diana and Mary Rivers, and Maria Temple, whose broad, clear brow reflects her moral nature, is named for intellect and rectitude.

The place names are similarly resonant: Gateshead, from where Jane's career issues forth; Lowood, where she must shelter and lie low as she acquires that prerequisite for independence, an education; Thornfield, a place of passion and suffering, casting a passing glance at another passion, of a more exulted kind, where a crown of thorns was the mockery of the victor's wreath; Whitcross, the real and metaphorical crossroads of Jane's life as she tears herself from the false paradise offered by her bigamous lover, and goes into lonely exile in the wilderness; Moor House, where, as a student pointed out, Jane gets *more*; and Ferndean Manor, which provides the bowery sanctuary for her happy-ever-after.

This quick sprint through the names has leap-frogged a key character: the fittingly named Helen Burns. Helen, from the Greek for light, lightens Jane's moral obscurity. Burns is for the cleansing of the martyr's fire and the Scottish stream. Helen is the martyr whose death serves as a beacon to light Jane's way ahead. Before Helen's influence, Jane was a mere passionate child; she had risen in desperate revolt against her tormentors at Gateshead, but was soon subdued:

> A ridge of lighted heath, alive, glancing, devouring, would have been a meet emblem of my mind when I accused and menaced Mrs. Reed: the same ridge, black and blasted after the flames are dead, would have represented as meetly my subsequent condition, when half an hour's silence and reflection had shown me the madness of my conduct, and the dreariness of my hated and hating position.
>
> (*Jane Eyre*, ch. 4)

In Helen, Charlotte presents moral fortitude, clear-sighted conviction, constant faith. Helen is totally alone; as alone as Jane herself. She faces suffering, humiliation and death. Her final words, however, are loving and joyful: 'God is my father; God is my friend: I love Him; I believe He loves me' (*Jane Eyre*, ch. 9).

Certainly, we are invited to see in Helen Burns the idealized image of Charlotte's own little mother; her sister, Maria, killed by neglect and indifference, if not active cruelty, at the infamous Cowan Bridge School attended by the four eldest Brontë sisters at the tenderest age. According to Charlotte's own report, Maria provided the model for Helen Burns, and she denied exaggerating her sister's patience and fortitude under the tyrant's yoke. The character of Helen Burns is crucial to the meaning of the novel. Charlotte invites us to consider: wherein lies strength and the power to triumph? Not in physical strength. Not in worldly considerations such as family, friends and fortune. Not in beauty and the superficial ability to charm and amuse. Not in age and maturity; some never live to acquire these traits.

And the answer? Strength is in resignation. Power comes through education. Triumph comes through the tutored spirit and moral courage. Resignation never becomes Jane's forte, but the rest is there in shining clarity: education, the tutored spirit, moral courage. And if English lessons cannot deal with issues such as these, let us go home now.

Why should we study *Jane Eyre*? Is there such a thing as a canon of literature that every educated person should know? Well yes, there is; and *Jane Eyre* is on the list. The only way to find out why is to read it. That is a safe line for the teacher of unquenched enthusiasm: 'What I know, delights me; it will delight you too.'

But what about the National Curriculum, the GCSE syllabus and the monstrous paraphernalia of weighing and measuring that has brought Dickens's satire in *Hard Times* to life in our times? Can *Jane Eyre* be taught at GCSE? Yes. For example, the NEAB course taught in my school includes a wider reading coursework unit on pre-twentieth-century prose. A nineteenth-century novel can be compared with a twentieth-century text (another novel, or a short story, for example) in terms of theme, genre or structure. *Jane Eyre* is wonderfully flexible on genre, interesting on education, gives vivid insights into the female mind, and is a first-person narrative. Enough there to match the book with several stock-cupboard standards. There is plenty of scope for close textual study: my very favourite passage is when Mr Brocklehurst catechizes young Jane:

'And what is hell? Can you tell me that?'
'A pit full of fire.'
'And should you like to fall into that pit, and to be burning there for ever?'
'No, sir.'

'What must you do to avoid it?'
I deliberated a moment: my answer, when it did come, was objectionable:
'I must keep in good health, and not die.'

(*Jane Eyre*, ch. 4)

By a quirk of fate I answered my door one day in London, to be confronted by that almost identical question put to me by passing evangelists: 'How do you feel about burning in eternal hell-fire?' My answer, like Jane's, was objectionable.

The sorrows and hardships of the Brontës' lives have blurred with the passing of time into a biography of matchless romanticism: the little orphans ('Oh, my poor children!' sighed Mrs Brontë as she died); the horrors of Cowan Bridge School and further bereavement; the struggle to succeed as teachers; the broken hearts; Branwell gone to the bad; Charlotte all alone; late love; pregnancy; premature death. On the face of it, the Brontës present a literary enigma: why weren't they dull, mousy prigs? How could these cold-climate virgins produce master-pieces of sexual passion? The Byronic heroes of *Jane Eyre* and *Wuthering Heights* have been the photofits for a million female fantasies. Yes, even schoolteachers of mature years will admit, if pressed, to being in love with Mr Rochester.

The enigma does, of course, unravel on closer study: there was very little that was ordinary about the Brontë sisters, and, when Charlotte made friends outside the family circle, she found other extraordinary women. Take, for example, her friend Mary Taylor, who travelled to New Zealand, made her fortune, and came back home again. A single woman in the middle years of the nineteenth century, of no rank or fortune, but armed with the kind of strength of character and physical courage that would still impress today.

Charlotte and her small circle were brave, determined women who have the power to inspire their modern great-great-granddaughters. They valued self-discipline: they buckled it on like moral armour each morning with their stays. I commend them to my students as worthy role models.

It is a good idea to invite students, from time to time, to consider what they are doing and why they are doing it. The answer to 'Why are you taking driving lessons?' is generally blindingly obvious. The answer to 'Why are you studying English literature?' may be less so. Literature supplies a longing in the human heart and mind. We are driven to look into the lives of others, to know them, to feel with them, to understand their world as we struggle to understand our own. Most students can articulate this before Key Stage 4. The next question is 'What have you read that was really good?' Then, 'Are there some works which every educated person should know?' The list which the student produces is not my list, needless to say, but, come to that, the student's own list will be different in a year or two. A good test of the success of a Key Stage 4 text is to ask a second-year A-level student what books she enjoyed lower down the school. I am happy to report the words 'Oh, I really loved that book!' have often been applied to *Jane Eyre* in these circumstances.

A good discussion on the subject of the literary canon and 'why study this book?' leads on to the question, 'What is art?' and theories of inspiration. The artist may well be spinning with silk from her own self, like the spider, but always, in the greatest acts of creation, there is the Higher Power at work. The muse acts through the artist and the result bears the mark of true life: not Dr Frankenstein's travesty but life in all its beauty and with the power of propagation. No work has better demonstrated the power of propagation than *Jane Eyre*: the only true begetter of a thousand romantic novels, not to mention the poetic and suggestive masterpiece, *Wide Sargasso Sea.*

Time to mention *Rebecca*, Daphne du Maurier's cracking yarn that begins with the evocation of the burnt out ruins of Thornfield-Manderley and rolls out an updated if not exactly dumbed down version of Jane Eyre's career. The other self is not raving in the attic, but plaguing the marriage in a more modern, psychological way. For all its sophistication, the unbridled sexuality of the first Mrs de Winter is not a million miles from the grovelling beast that is the first Mrs Rochester: 'The maniac bellowed: she parted her shaggy locks from her visage, and gazed wildly at her visitors. I recognized well that purple face – those bloated features.' Mr Rochester's comment makes the point explicit: 'Such is the sole conjugal embrace I am ever to know' (*Jane Eyre*, ch. 26).

In this episode, Rochester invites his audience to contrast two extremes of female sexuality:

> 'This is my wife . . . And this is what I wished to have' (laying his hand on my shoulder): 'this young girl, who stands so grave and quiet at the mouth of hell.'

Jane herself has earlier set before her reader a similar comparison, between herself and Blanche: 'the contrast was as great as self-control could desire' (*Jane Eyre*, ch. 16). Daphne du Maurier's Maxim de Winter, with his mysterious, even criminal past, is clearly intended as a dominant Byronic hero in the same mould as Mr Rochester. The unnamed narrator, the second Mrs de Winter, is certainly a toned down, mousier version of Jane. The moral absolutes of Charlotte's book have, predictably perhaps, dwindled into the moral relatives and compromises of the twentieth century: Mr Rochester redeems his sins by laying down his right arm and his sight for the wife who has blighted his life; Maxim tells a load of lies and gets away with something approaching murder.

> Edward Fairfax Rochester; we love you! We love you because you are our mirrored selves; a girl's dream. The scene for the fateful meeting is set with care: the brooklet is 'congealed' with ice. 'The rising moon' is 'pale as a cloud, but brightening momently'. In the silence, Jane tells us, 'my ear too felt the flow of currents'.
>
> (*Jane Eyre*, ch. 12)

As she paced the leads of Thornfield, Jane had longed for: 'the busy world, towns, regions full of life I had heard of but never seen' (*Jane Eyre*, ch. 12). Now, the busy world bursts in upon her silent, frozen life:

> A rude noise broke on these fine ripplings and whisperings, at once so far away and so clear: a positive tramp, tramp, a metallic clatter, which effaced the soft wave-wanderings; as, in a picture, the solid mass of a crag, or the rough boles of a great oak, drawn in dark and strong in the foreground, efface the aerial distance of azure hill, sunny horizon, and blended clouds, where tint melts into tint.
>
> (*Jane Eyre*, ch. 12)

Now, there's a good episode for close textual study. The preceding passage is full of diction to do with the silent, frozen state of both landscape and heroine's heart. Mr Rochester's advent is full of diction of noise and vigour. A little deft use of the highlighter reveals the author's method. And, no doubt, Freud would have a comment to make, too.

Fate brings Rochester, in all his pounding vigour and masculinity, crashing to the heroine's feet: 'Man and horse were down; they had slipped on the sheet of ice which glazed the causeway' (*Jane Eyre*, ch. 12). This is a delicious premonition of what is to follow. Mr Rochester may be Jane's superior in rank and fortune; he is certainly her inferior in terms of the tutored spirit, the moral soul. Before the pair can come together as equals Jane must acquire family and fortune, and, more significantly, Rochester must atone, must find moral redemption. The unicorn must lay its head humbly in the lap of the stainless maiden.

The secret of Mr Rochester's success as a romantic hero lies in his ability to *know* Jane. The physical charms of Blanche Ingram ('the august yet harmonious lineaments, the Grecian neck and bust ... the round and dazzling arm ... the delicate hand,' as Jane imagines her, with a distinctly sour tone, in Chapter 16) cannot compete in Rochester's eyes with the 'Governess, disconnected, poor, and plain', who tells him with passionate conviction: 'It is my spirit that addresses your spirit; just as if both had passed through the grave, and we stood at God's feet, equal – as we are!' (*Jane Eyre*, ch. 23). That is the mark of the ideal lover. He is not beguiled by wiles and artifice. He sees into her unique soul and finds there his redemptive twin, *his better half*: 'You – poor and obscure, and small and plain as you are – I entreat to accept me as a husband' (*Jane Eyre*, ch. 23).

As with Heathcliff and Cathy, Rochester and Jane share a transcendent union. However, both Brontë heroes are also embodiments of virile force and ardour. Remember how Jane pours scorn on the cold, sexless love offered by St John Rivers:

> ... forced to keep the fire of my nature continually low, to compel it to burn inwardly and never utter a cry, though the imprisoned flame consumed vital after vital – *this* would be unendurable.
>
> (*Jane Eyre*, ch. 34)

St John cannot *know* Jane; cannot truly assess her peculiar worth; enter her private, internal life. That's what Jane means by love. It is also what Cathy was getting at when she said: 'I *am* Heathcliff' (*Wuthering Heights*, ch. 9).

Both Heathcliff and Rochester are female fantasies. Rochester can, at times, be cruel and domineering, though his sadism stops far short of Heathcliff's worst excesses. Both are imperilled spirits, redeemed at last by union with their twin souls. Heathcliff wins his love through suffering and death, Rochester through self-sacrifice and mutilation. The hero is depicted as physically powerful, well travelled, rich and worldly. Other women seek his attention through fashionable display and feminine wiles, but he despises them. He has met his heart's desire and knew her instantly. His love is sealed for ever.

Jean Rhys's Mr Rochester is of a different order of psychological depth and reality. His narrative shows us Antoinette through the mists of his own fear, alienation and self-disgust. We see his cold-hearted, ruthless refusal to see clearly his suffering wife or hear her pleas for pity and love. He has only the power to crush; not the power to love, to liberate, to *know* another. The story is harrowing and credible.

Charlotte's Rochester is an essential element of the moral structure of the work. He is Jane's temptation, and, ultimately, her saviour. He tempts her to throw away her *self*: her name, her independent identity. Then, when his bigamous secret is revealed, he tempts her to throw away her good name, her moral being. He pleads, he demands, he threatens to damn his own soul by suicide and lay the blame at her door. Jane must tear her heart and body out of Thornfield, into the wilderness, where she wanders friendless and hungry, without roof or hearth. Benign Providence guides Jane to the wicket gate and beckoning lamp of her true sisters; the women of intellect and refinement seeking independence through education.

Now temptation returns in the form of Rochester's mirror image, the icy fanatic, St John Rivers. St John pleads and demands, as Rochester did, that Jane surrender to his will; this time Jane is told that God Himself requires her submission: 'consider my offer; and do not forget that if you reject it, it is not me you deny, but God' (*Jane Eyre*, ch. 34). Jane's initial reply – 'I scorn your idea of love ... I scorn the counterfeit sentiment you offer: yes, St. John, and I scorn you when you offer it' – echoes her childish act of self-assertion in the face of Aunt Reed's tyranny:

> 'I shall remember how you thrust me back – roughly and violently thrust me back – into the red-room, and locked me up there ... you are bad; hard-hearted. You are deceitful!'
>
> (*Jane Eyre*, ch. 4)

Jane has escaped from the confinement of the red-room: childish powerlessness, financial dependence, friendlessness. She has known love. Her dearly won liberty is not to be relinquished easily. However, St John has struck a raw nerve: Jane's sense of duty and of moral destiny.

At this crucial point re-enter Mr Rochester, transmuted from tempter to saviour. His call comes in answer to Jane's prayer: ' "Show me, show me the path!" I entreated of Heaven' (*Jane Eyre*, ch. 35). The mystic response is in Rochester's voice: 'Jane! Jane! Jane!'

Charlotte does not show with dramatic immediacy the fiery climax of retribution: Thornfield in flames, Mr Rochester's heroic figure silhouetted on the rooftop as he struggles to save his tormentor, the wife who has robbed him of his youth and innocence. The drama is long over when Jane hears of it, and she finds Mr Rochester morally elevated but unquenched: 'He looked and spoke with earnestness: his old impetuosity was rising. "We must become one flesh without any delay, Jane" ' (*Jane Eyre*, ch. 37).

In the Ferndean episode there is a playful rerun of the earlier comparisons between Jane and first Blanche, then Bertha. This time, Mr Rochester compares himself to St John Rivers:

> 'Your words have delineated very prettily a graceful Apollo: he is present to your imagination – tall, fair, blue-eyed, and with a Grecian profile. Your

eyes dwell on a Vulcan – a real blacksmith, brown, broad-shouldered; and blind and lame into the bargain.'

(Jane Eyre, ch. 37)

The tables turned, indeed!

Jane's response is unequivocal:

'Mr. Rochester, if ever I did a good deed in my life – if ever I thought a good thought – if ever I prayed a sincere and blameless prayer – if ever I wished a righteous wish – I am rewarded now. To be your wife is, for me, to be as happy as I can be on earth.'

(Jane Eyre, ch. 37)

Art has its origins in religion: once, when the musician played, the dancer moved, the artist marked the rock or the poet sang, it was for God alone. Charlotte was aiming at a wider audience. Nevertheless, her book has a strength of purpose and nobility that fixes it in the finest artistic tradition. The aim in teaching any great text is not to transmit the massive gleanings of a lifetime's study, but just to open a door for the student. Charlotte has created a compelling love-story in the best rags-to-riches tradition. Symbol and thematic imagery provide a powerful poetic subtext. The structure is built on the classic simplicity of life-as-a-journey, pointing the way with names loaded with allegorical significance. These aspects of the book are readily accessible to the Key Stage 4 student.

Once the door is open, *Jane Eyre* walks in.

Chapter 5

'The Difference to Be Shared'
Some aspects of the work of Gillian Clarke

John Richardson

I first came across the work of Gillian Clarke when I was doing some A-Level examination marking for the Associated Examination Board a few years ago. It was the Unseen Poetry paper and one of the unseen poems set for comment was bringing out writing of a much higher standard in the set of papers I was marking than any piece of writing, poetry or prose that I had marked for several years. The poem was called 'Miracle on St. David's Day' and came from a volume of poems called *Letter from a Far Country* by Gillian Clarke.

For some reason, this poem touched a chord with a new generation of readers, something perhaps to do with that sigh of relief in an examination when you recognize that 'you know this one'. Most of the candidates had immediately made the link with another poem they 'knew' – Wordsworth's famous poem 'The Daffodils', from which Clarke had helpfully (especially if you're sitting in an examination room) included two lines as a superscription – but as much to do with the poem's integrity and humanity, and with the power of poetry itself: its capacity to touch nerve-ends and unlock closed minds, especially in the portrait of the labourer in 'Miracle on St. David's Day' rocking gently to the rhythms of Wordsworth's verses which we imagine he had learned in the sanity and security of his childhood.

Here there were links for candidates, many of whom, I guess, had looked forward to that morning's exam with a mixture of half-hearted hope and despair: 'unseen poetry!' And yet here they were being given hope, both within the poem itself and for themselves as candidates: they could even, and not only the best of them, make valuable cross-referenced comparisons by way of explaining their thinking; comparisons which arose naturally from their own limited experience of poetry and not those comparisons forced upon them and their teachers because of some strange, centralized National Curriculum reductive dogmatism that demands works of poetry and prose to be read in pairs and compared and contrasted, as though that were the main purpose and justification for their existence as works of literature. These candidates had understood something and had real and personal things to say, and that is a godsend when you are examining two or three hundred scripts.

It is worth saying here that examination marking is to my mind one of the best and quickest routes by which any teacher, especially a young teacher, can improve the relevance of his or her classroom syllabus teaching technique. Not only does it allow you to gain valuable insights into the thought processes of senior examiners – and in my experience these are people with a keen interest in the subject – it also offers you a view of examinations which is much less institutional and much more personal than you would otherwise come to expect. There are unlooked-for benefits here too: it can prompt you to read beyond those texts which you might not instinctively pick off the bookshelves.

The poem in question(!), 'Miracle on St. David's Day', from the volume, *Letter from a Far Country*, prompted me to look out for more poems by Gillian Clarke and I came across the slim, orange-covered volume, *The Sundial*. For a time I considered Clarke as a private discovery, and in some ways I consider that she still is. I say this in spite of the fact that she has been on at least two examination syllabuses in recent years, at A-Level and GCSE, and that her *Collected Poems* lists more than a hundred and thirty poems, but she seems still not to be given the attention that her work demands.

Oddly, for example, she does not even warrant a mention in *The New Poetry*, published in 1993, and she barely gets a mention in our most recent British and Irish poetry anthologies: Sean O'Brien's *The Firebox* (Picador) includes 'Llyr', a poem chosen with his typical perspicacity and sure touch, which brings to me, at least, a new dimension to Shakespeare's tragedy *King Lear* – King Lear? ... Welsh? ... 'Llyr'? ... why was I never told this? And this is no idle question. For the poem starts from different ground, from different national assumptions, and brought a new insight to me as teacher, playgoer and reader; as an *English* reader. I have taught *King Lear* many times. I know him as a British chieftain; I have made assumptions about the role of Cornwall, but in absorbing the rudiments of the play I have translated it on to 'home' ground, somewhere not very clearly defined in my mind, somewhere around Middle England: Gloucestershire or Worcestershire, I suppose, and in so doing have been guilty of some sort of literary colonialism. This new view of the play, coming from the West, set the cultural compass spinning in realignment. But there is much more to this poem as well. This is a poem about the magic that the power of language holds for children; the specialness and excitement to be found in the early learning of individual words; the grip it has on the minds of the young, boys (let us not forget this) as well as girls. This poem reasserts (should it be needed, and it probably does) a reassuring justification for introducing the best of our tradition of drama to the young, even though we may not see any directly measurable effects at the time. In their weighty anthology, *The Penguin Book of Poetry from Britain and Ireland since 1945*, Armitage and Crawford include only two poems by Gillian Clarke, and you can see how one of these, 'Overheard in County Sligo', got in there. For this poem is recognizably in the tradition of W. B. Yeats, with its echoes of 'The Lake Isle of Innisfree'.

I intend to pick up later other associations and developments which hark back to Yeats's works. The tone and matter of these lines, along with a reference to the Abbey Theatre, Dublin, suggest the sort of deliberate homage to Yeats that any anthologist can feel secure about. Its inclusion in this anthology says a lot about the ways in which we look at poetry, but it doesn't say, or perhaps seek to say, much about the corpus of Clarke's work, and in some ways it delimits its breadth, vigour and range.

Gillian Clarke does, however, make it into the Oxford poetry list volume *Six Women Poets*, and in good company too, and this perhaps gives a clue about why she has for some time, to my mind, been marginalized: she can be seen by those who do not know her work as coming from the borders of literature, or, as she recognizes with pride, from a far country: Wales itself, but more especially, 'womanhood'.

There is no doubt that being 'Welsh and a woman' still places you in a far country. The centre of literary gravity still seems to reside in male, suburban, southeast England, even though we have come a long way since Clarke felt, as she recalls in *Poets on Poets*, that she had needed to come to feel 'permitted' to write poetry in the first place by reading the writings of the Brontë sisters.

Furthermore, I still see her described by editors and commentators (I can think of one in particular on the shelves of our English Department stock cupboard) as writing in defence of 'feminist' values, which she might well do, but that single description of one, albeit vital aspect of her writing has never seemed to me to be entirely or even mainly appropriate to what she has to say, nor to the range and development of her writing. However, I guess that at one time this sort of publicity could be directed to attract some potential readers who might have been keen to pick up a poet whom they could regard as a polemicist and feminist apologist.

To consider her work only in those terms would be to do her a massive injustice. Clarke's is a loving voice which speaks with understanding as she seeks to adjust to a new position and to help men, '... husbands, fathers, forefathers ...', to accommodate to new and perhaps discomforting realities.

> this is ...
> my bottle in the sea which might
> take a generation to arrive.
>
> 'Letter from a Far Country'

That bottle has splintered on the shores of many family lives since this poem was written, leaving men to seek new ways of finding an identity which does not rely upon job and workplace status. The turmoil which has wrecked and reshaped family lives and especially the lives of the men within the family was foreshadowed in 'East Moors'.

These experiences have been repeated up and down 'quieter, cleaner, poorer' Full Monty Britain, and the bitterness of the East Moors men becomes a metaphor and symbol for wasted lives in which the sole redeeming feature is the love and resourcefulness that the women supply, as they have supplied it for generations, and we begin to see the gentle irony at work in the far country.

Clarke constantly returns to her roots in Wales in her writing: to her family, to her threshold and home, and to the woman's vital place within all three. She tells us in the same poem, 'East Moors', of how she lives in the house where she was born, and we get to know this house of her childhood through many different poems across many books: her room in the roof, the whiteness of its ceiling, shadowed and 'freckled' with sea light and lamplight.

Home: the house and garden. The place of the family; the past generations of that family, bedrock of lives today, echoing lives lived in that place across the generations: her grandmother hanging out the family's washing which is lifted, then as now, by the winds from the sea.

This unreal garden from the past might well be the garden of 'The Sundial' where a healing and a growth of understanding happen between mother and son as he creates a paper sundial on the grass. And it might also be the garden where her daughter, in sundress and shorts, rocks on the swing, pushing away from her mother, for the time being, on this garden swing, returning this time (and perhaps for always), on love's pendulum. Thus, commonplace locations and domestic activities are the starting points where she records with close observation the tensions between parents and children. Voicing the risks and fears which lie at the very heart of maternal and family love, the fears of separation and of the emotional vacancy that comes with the thought of losing touch with the children you have brought into this world. This is powerfully expressed in 'Sailing'.

> ... I felt
> As though on the water he had found
> New ways of evasion, a sheet
> Of icy water to roll out between us.

There is a heartening maturity of feeling here. How special it is to catch such moments in our closest relationships. I recognize the gripping feelings that are there; I have felt them as a father and can only imagine the extra intensity that a mother would feel, and the wealth of emotional generosity that goes into letting go. So much of Clarke's poetry is written with the motive of sharing.

This sharing transcends generations. In one poem, the sonnet 'Marged', Clarke takes us back to an imagined past in the same house, where a previous owner, the eponymous Marged, is brought before us again, living a hard life '... alone in winter, ill and penniless'.

The place is the same place generations on, but the lives of these two women are very different. One thing brings them together, as Clarke sees it, their womanhood: the elemental, intrinsic state of being a woman in this place transcends the changes in time, just as it will overcome the ravages that post-industrialism will force upon the families.

Clarke is fortunate to have an archive of family history, a literary and poetic archive to sustain her. We meet this distinctly Welsh poetic form of biography in the long poem 'Confiant', which describes something of this genealogy of family by letting us meet again its members from the past. There must be possibilities for teachers here; a new slant on the 'Autobiographies' that make up part of the English curriculum at some key stage or other. It is in this poem that we find what I consider to be one of the key tenets of Clarke's philosophical outlook:

> Do they know, who live there,
> how I tread the loose tile in the hall,
> feel for the light the wrong side of the door,
> add my prints to their prints to my old prints
> on the finger-plate?

There is a descriptive corollary at work throughout the poem that reflects this idea of transcendence. The idea will be familiar to readers of

Yeats. Yeats was an admirer of Berkeley, the philosopher, and you can catch some of the elements of this philosophy in Clarke's work, especially in the major poem 'Letter from a Far Country'.

The first two of Berkeley's 'Seven Propositions' are:

> Reality is a timeless and spaceless community of Spirits which perceive each other. Each Spirit is determined by and determines those it perceives and each Spirit is unique.

and

> When these Spirits reflect themselves in time and space, they still determine each other and each Spirit sees the other as thoughts, images, objects of sense, Time and space are unreal.

It might be poetic instinct or it could well be that Clarke is thinking of this when she writes about the whispering voices in the wells and woodlands:

> All their old conversations
> collected carefully, faded
> and difficult to read, yet held
> forever as voices in a well.
>
> 'Letter from a Far Country'

It probably has much to do with the prevailing silence within which the poem's letter is written and, in a more sublime way, more difficult to analyse, something to do with Clarke's cryptic belief that 'Much is said by leaving the rest unsaid' (Quoted in *Six Women Poets* (OUP)) in the sense, I believe, that she thinks our spirits and those of previous generations commune silently with each other, 'determine each other and are determined by each other'. The presences of the 'dead' generations of forefathers and foremothers are unseen, but are all around us. We catch half-glimpses of them and hear their (and our) whispers, perhaps, and a poet is more able than others to interpret the significance of these voices.

In 'Letter from a Far Country', the poet sees the need to respond to these voices; the duty we have to write back and share the communication and the communion. The responsibility that the poet as daughter bears to the past is akin to the responsibility the poet as mother bears to the future. Things only exist in being perceived, and the poet is personally and particularly equipped to perceive presences and existences. Yeats said that Berkeley had 'brought us back the world that only exists because it shines and sounds'. Look at the recurring references to light shining off the surfaces of Clarke's writing:

> The silence resettles
> slowly as dust on the sunlit
> surfaces of the furniture.
>> 'Letter from a Far Country'

Light and sound. The poet starts with 'this perfectly white page' and the art is to catch and express the sounds and reflections from the surfaces of the world. The sheer intensity of the sensual imagery deepens the effect of her experiences and recalls the work of French symbolists: 'Listen! to the starlings glistening.' The internal rhyme in the line itself achieves a sparkle of its own to correspond with the glistening of the starlings shining feathers. There are many references in this poem to the light of surfaces, and to silences and 'noises', and they build together into a complex pattern of communion which is one of the features of the letter. For what is a letter if it is not a sharing? However, we learn at the end of the poem that this letter, once written, is never sent; much is said by leaving the rest unsaid.

The concentration upon these intensities of light continues through into the later poems. 'Estuary' in *Five Fields* works through an abstraction of images which flash and dazzle at first and then reveal a more solid and common significance, while 'The Habit of Light' illuminates a woman whose existence is held clearly in this poem of loving reflection:

> her red hair bright
> with her habit of colour, her habit of light.

This is artistry which I admire, the revelation of layers of existence and the sharing of perceptions which try to put us in closer touch with the sheer wonder of what we so often dismiss as the everyday world around us. Then there is the blindingly sunny day which is the setting for the suggestive relationships half hinted at in 'Return to Login', a 'brilliance' that turns again with a typical switch of image which moves the reader back through time:

> Should he turn now to wave and wait
> for me, where sunlight concentrates
> blindingly on this bridge, he'd see
> all this in sepia, hear her footsteps
> not yet taken fade away.

This is modern, this juggling with the possibilities of time and language so that the juxtaposing of the events presented makes them appear both to seem to have happened and yet to be about to happen. We have moved on some way from Yeats, and it would be wrong to suggest that Clarke's work represents some clumsy second-hand pastiche of Yeats's poems. It is more that those images she has come across in the locality and topicality of her own experience of life hold for her something of the same representational appeal that they held for Yeats.

Certainly, I feel safe saying this about the emblematic significance of water. The employment and exploration of water imagery is elemental to her thinking and writing. We have met this in Yeats, and it too has its corollary in the idea of transcendence; of generations in their life journeys: we, the living, the dead, and those to come. The River Mellte drops underground and flows through limestone caves, reminding us of the waters of Coole Park and Ballylee running through dark Raftery's cellar and dropping underground to rise again in Coole demesne, the journey taking on for Yeats the significance of the journey of the 'generated soul'.

Clarke feels a 'pity' for 'rivers inside mountains'. There is a running emblem/image of water in her work too. The 'big sea running in a shell' becomes the pulsing blood in her skull. The seals in the seas beyond her back garden and the cormorants 'snaking underneath the surfaces' are unseen but still present, just as in some metaphorical way the spirits of the previous living remain present but unseen. We catch only glimpses, hear only their whisperings coming from woodlands or in the songs of non-existent birds which 'ring like a tambourine' or they ripple on in the waters and wellsprings of our lives: 'held/forever as voices in a well.'

There is an arterial resourcefulness running through the imagery of Clarke's writing and thinking, the river bearing the communal memory, the deep subconscious as it bears the rains of the past weeks. We see this in the poem 'Hölderlin in Tubingen' and in 'Rain', where the garden soaks up the downpours which soak deep into the porous shale until they reach the bedrock, a source of life for future generations. And always, always, the verse makes links with home, garden and family love.

This love and affection runs as deep as the well-water in a poem rich with smells, music, warmth and light. Its tone is very different from 'Elegy', where a similar imagery quenches a grief over the death of a close person, her mother, I suspect:

> Each glassful is archaeology,
> brimmed seepings
> that have taken life-times to collect.

Here are the unifying features of her poetry: the closeness of family and of the wife, mother, daughter, sister within it; the continuum of existences, personal and human, across time; the images drawn from the local and the particular.

If you do not know her work, this might make it sound esoteric, narrow and old-fashioned. Far from it. In its form and content the poetry is varied, often innovative and experimental, and most of all, it is a poetry which stays in touch. If you are a teacher it offers examples of varieties of form and style: there are traditional forms, sonnets, ballads, elegiac verse, narratives; there are traditional Welsh forms.

There are also more innovative and experimental forms. 'Found poetry', for example, in lists taken from Parish Books, or simple recipe lists for home-baked bread, or a familiar fragment from the script of a weather forecast, caught, I guess, on a radio during a long car journey (one of many journeys recalled in the poems). Along with the found poetry there are other risky innovations; parenthetical asides and comments, for example, in 'Letter from a Far Country', sometimes deliberately prosaic:

> (You'll find my inventories pinned
> inside all of the cupboard doors)

and sometimes more mysterious and evocative:

> If you hear your name in that talk
> don't listen. Eavesdroppers never
> heard anything good of themselves.

Then there is the device of deliberately switching forms and fonts within a poem in order to achieve a particular effect, as at the end of 'Letter from a Far Country'. Here, Clarke employs a traditional ballad form set as a series of questions making up the last three stanzas. This variation of font styles in the poem is also characteristic, seen performing a different poetic function in 'Siege', where the shift to italics lifts us back in time to a world photographed in her babyhood. Then there are the esoteric, difficult and unexpected ways in which she handles metaphor and imagery with a mobility which takes you by surprise as it adopts an idea and shifts it on without warning, spinning one image into another: circles of water which a few lines later become 'a collar of water' around the neck of a seal and, a few lines after that, golden corn encircling a tree in the middle of a field.

Such shifts and continually developing images are ever-present. It is almost as if Clarke is suspicious of any poetic mood which allows or persuades her and us to take completely seriously our traditional expectations of the verse: the assumptions are subversive; you cannot afford to relax.

Don't doubt, however, that she can write beautifully evocative and effective pastoral descriptions when the need is evident, but she has a habit of twisting a theme once established. The reader is unsettled, and forced to revisit assumptions and expectations. This is why a Coca-Cola can will suddenly bob into our consciousness once the visionary and emblematic have been set so strongly in the verse and why 'windows curtained with flame' later 'catch, not fire, but/the setting sun'.

Then there is the local colour: real people, members of her family, her children, her ancestors; local names and members of the Parish, alive and long dead; snatches of the Welsh (her first) language and of real conversations (we are led to believe) are all included in the body of her poetry whenever it is significant; modern commercial names like Yamaha and Coca-Cola meet trademarks of older generations like Brasso to add a touch of realism or, more subtly, sometimes used to break the spell of a vision or image. We share in the life of this close community by virtue of a poetry where images of sharing dominate: sharing relationships; sharing a common humanity or sexuality, even or especially across years and generations; sharing a grief; sharing a job, a house, a sense of each other's lives and each other's emotional states: anger and rage, contemplation, threat, elation, grief, compassion, innocence and love. The lines and journeys of these shared communications are emphatically present, be they emotional, symbolic or concrete. This poetry sets out to put us in touch with the world around us. It does so from the security of the wellsprings fed by a profound consideration of the experiences that life has brought her and by her insights and sympathy for the lives that others lived before her. This is not a narrow, nationalistic poetry. There is pride in the love of her home parish, but the world beyond is ever-present, however long the lines of communication, and this world is a darker world, and a darker, much more threatening tone can develop in the verse as the child's understanding grows and learns. Rumours of war, space exploration and a 'strange red dust' invade and disturb the local Welsh world. The poetry here, in 'Siege', for example, is marked by swiftly changing images, a breathless confusion, a destructive energy which refutes passivity. There is political maturity and the assumption of responsibility for future lives.

The later work in *Five Fields* picks up this theme from the very beginning: the smallness of the globe which we inhabit. The Parish is no longer only a Welsh parish; it is now a world, and this world, too, is 'so little'. The communicating routes are now as likely to be main roads and airlines as much as rivers and rain. Distances are travelled; journeys completed; connections made, and we are constantly confronted by the difficulty of how to absorb into our local lives the moral iniquities which we hear of on the daily news broadcasts. Bosnian bullet holes; the 'horror of Saddleworth moor' urban terrorism. Brutality real and artistic, recorded in the unspeakable portrayal of mass death in an art installation by Anthony Gormley. All these experiences force us to recognize our common humanity, and to express the need to share the suffering of the victims of modern life. The poem 'The Field Mouse' also imposes this moral problem upon us. A dead field-mouse is brought to her by a child and prompts nightmares in which

> ... the children dance in the grass,
> their bones as brittle as mouse-ribs, the air
> stammering with gun-fire, my neighbour turns
> stranger, wounding my land with stones.

The family fields are warm in the summer sunshine but we are none of us immune from the violence that threatens our neighbours, and it doesn't matter whether they are next door, at the other end of a motorway, in the Balkans or on the other side of the world. How can we find ways to connect these indescribably bloody violations with the routine banalities of our everyday lives?

We live in violent times. In 'The Bomb', it is Manchester that has suffered a bomb outrage: the lines scan across a slow-motion movie poem of a madness in which

> Glass hangs in the air, scarves, tee-shirts,
> flowers, newspapers, Kleenex ...

They are so simple and ordinary, these bits and pieces of local shopping-centre life. It leaves us unsettled, this close-up blitz of images. The enormity of this bomb-burst cracks apart the rhythm of the poem itself, and we are left with a repetitive litany of bewilderment, grief, rage and reconstruction. What matters here, as in so many of her poems, is the way in which the poet can invest the phenomenal with a significance that will carry the event beyond the local to the universal.

Setting about teaching a poet, or any writer that you admire, at Key Stage 4 is much more difficult now than at any time I can remember. It is not so much the actual classroom practice which makes it difficult, or what some would see, mistakenly I think, as a 'natural resistance to poetry', especially, on the part of 15-year-olds; it is simply that the Key

Stage 4 curriculum is so crowded and constrained that the professional freedom of a teacher to choose works that she or he thinks might interest the class has almost disappeared in state schools, and my recent experience leads me to believe that this affects the personal control over classwork and the proper professional discretion which we ought to accord our young teachers most of all. But it is still this personal vision of writing that makes the job worthwhile, and it is because of this that it is well worth breaking away from the examination coursework whenever you can in order to chase your own enthusiasms with your class.

In fact, Clarke does turn up on syllabus lists now and again. NEAB recently offered a small selection of her work, and she is well received in the classroom, allowing different approaches and demonstrating different poetic techniques.

There is no doubt in my mind that poetry is best taught as an oral lesson. I have increasingly come to use an overhead projector in my teaching (OHP) because it enables you to face the group and engage them while adding their ideas and contributions to the OHP sheet which will be immediately projected on to the wall behind you. Most schools have a few spare OHPs lying idle and under-used in stock cupboards, especially as the newer technologies attract more attention, and they are a godsend and little appreciated for, with an OHP, students see at first hand, right before their eyes, what we mean when we say 'make notes' about a poem, since the teacher can write down the ideas as they are voiced on the 'overhead' alongside the poem.

There is so much in Clarke's work that instinctively interests adolescents. I mentioned 'Overheard in County Sligo' earlier and I think that this is a good poem to begin with, not only because it offers the chance of making the link with Yeats's work, but because the poem offers the chance of discussing the nature of a life philosophically: it is not only ex-football managers who are interested in the transmigration of souls, and noisy class discussions can arise out of the matter of this poem. It also gives you the opportunity to provide a historical context to the work.

Clarke's poems are about the lives we lead. Look at 'Last Rites' and 'The Bomb'. Give the class a pile of newspapers and work on these poems with the newspapers alongside, shaping words between them into a collage poem, with articles and items drawn both from the papers and the poems. This is a fail-safe way of getting a class to engage with the writing of any poet, practically, analytically and creatively, but Clarke's writing offers us some natural leads in this respect.

The poem which first acquainted me with the work of Gillian Clarke, 'Miracle on St. David's Day', provides a teacher with a chance to introduce Wordsworth by a natural association of context and opportunities to open discussion on human values, human rights and the ways in which poetry itself works upon us as individuals. This has always proved a sure choice to get children talking.

Most English department teaching programmes include 'Autobiography' somewhere at Key Stage 3 or 4, and I think it is a good teacher who encourages at least part of an autobiography to be written in verse. There are, of course, many literary antecedents to choose from, but Clarke's work is a good starting point. So much of it can show young writers how to elevate the ordinary, to find a subject for poetry in their own gardens, back streets or villages. They can see how the everyday experience can lead us into deeper thoughts about life and our place in a family or community; they can make an autobiography 'project' into a more profound and artistic piece of work. I indicated earlier in this chapter the variety of openings that can be found in 'Letter from a Far Country', although you would do best to choose your selected excerpts carefully, as this is a long and difficult poem for Key Stage 4 students.

That said, it is good to get children to 'copy' and emulate. In doing so, they learn the crafts of writing 'through the fingers', and I pointed out earlier the parts which make good starting points, especially the 'found' poetry. You might also take, for example, the structure of the poem 'My Box', in *Collected Poems*. I use this framework for creative poetry writing and it works well. It is a simple form, working through stanza by stanza, moving from the physical to the metaphorical in easy stages, and in my experience it seems to enable all students to end up with a page of 'poetry' that they will be proud of.

I find it slightly odd to be writing about a Welsh poet. I know only a few Welsh people, mostly men, teacher colleagues, all of them a bit larger than life and expressedly 'Welsh' in the south of England where I live. They strike me as people with a fragile joviality and a deep, well-hidden thoughtfulness. Good teachers, all of them.

I haven't been to Wales more than two or three times in my life. I hold no memories or childhood nostalgia to predispose me to Gillian Clarke's homeland except one, the memory of a significant and enduring coincidence which happened to me in Wales when I was taking a school canoeing trip down the River Wye.

I was on mini-bus shuttle duty and it was my turn after breakfast to leave the campsite and hitch a lift back the thirty miles or so to where we had left the bus the day before, at a place called the 'Tump'. The first lorry I thumbed that sunny morning picked me up. It was a beautiful day, late July, and when I was dropped off I felt like walking the next stretch of road. There was no one else about. I walked up a hill along a silent road, and as I came over the brow of the hill I was met by the sight of a red-stone ruined castle. Unbelievable. And, better still: right alongside the castle (it seems so, now, after many years) there was a pub . . . and it was open!

I sat in the summer sun, drinking a pint of beer, and only then realized this was all happening on my birthday. Sometimes life offers you small glimpses of magic.

I don't know if Gillian Clarke lives in the part of Wales where that happened, and to this day I don't know the name of the castle or the pub; I've never been back there since, but I find much of what I discovered that day in her poetry. Something to do with convergences; with touching deeper streams than we can fully know; evoking sources of energy and motion which come to as unexpectedly, and with much the same significance as the events of that birthday in Wales held for me, because it was limited and personal and yet it convinced me that I had arrived at some sort of crossroads in time.

This is a good time to be reading Gillian Clarke, and I am pleased that I have come across her poetry at a moment which might be one of the defining periods for her country. Her poetry offers us the possibilities of a deeper understanding of the wellsprings of a culture, of its history and its people's lives, especially the lives of its women; and an understanding of how it perceives itself and how it connects with the world beyond its borders.

Chapter 6

Twentieth-century Drama

Clare Middleton

It is clear from page 20 of the original version of *English in the National Curriculum,* which set out the range of literature to be taught at Key Stages 3 and 4, that drama was the genre which posed most problems for government education officials when they were drawing up lists of prescribed and suggested authors. Drama made two appearances in the original list: first as 'two plays by Shakespeare', and second as 'drama by major playwrights, e.g. Christopher Marlowe, J. B. Priestley, George Bernard Shaw, R. B. Sheridan'. It is interesting that these drama lists were not separated into pre-1900 and post-1900 works, unlike both the poetry and prose lists. The four suggested playwrights, who were presumably meant to represent all dramatic output from the Mystery Plays to the present day, sat rather apologetically alongside the far longer lists of pre-1900 poets and prose writers to be studied. Even the post-1900 lists managed seven suggestions for poetry and five for prose, the latter daringly even including a female writer.

The other significant difference between the drama and poetry/prose lists arose out of the National Curriculum's statement that 'Pupils should . . . read literature by major writers from earlier in the twentieth century and works of high quality by contemporary writers.' Contemporary authors were represented by Hughes and Heaney in the poetry list, and (rather less confidently) by Greene, Golding and Spark in the prose list. The nearest we came to a contemporary dramatist was J. B. Priestley. In the revised programmes of study, first published for consultation in the summer of 1999, this has, to some extent, been addressed. At the time of writing, Shaffer and Pinter now sit alongside Shaw and Wilde as 'major playwrights', and there is an entirely new section of 'new and contemporary drama' which includes Alan Ayckbourn, Alan Bennett, Brian Friel and Willy Russell. It is heartening to see that we may now teach the works of these wonderful modern writers with government approval, but disappointing that female playwrights are still conspicuous by their absence from the list. This could be rectified if the Qualifications and Curriculum Authority were to include more dramatists best known for their television writing rather than their stage writing. As I will go on to illustrate, television is a rich source of drama, and it could be argued that the study of television drama is at least as relevant as the study of theatre drama to the majority of students.

During the course of this chapter I will be considering the role of the twentieth-century drama text in the Key Stage 4 classroom. I will be arguing the importance of retaining a significant amount of drama text teaching in the Key Stage 4 curriculum. Throughout, I will shape my arguments around three key works by Willy Russell, focusing on their educational and literary value, the ways in which students respond to them, and what, in my experience, they gain from studying them. I will not be discussing Shakespeare. A close debate on the issues surrounding the teaching of Shakespeare in schools at Key Stage 4 merits an entirely separate chapter. I intend to focus on twentieth-century drama because I would like to examine the potential of such texts for enabling students to fully engage with ideas relating to the society in which they live as well as stimulating discussion about literary and linguistic aspects of the texts.

I begin with *Educating Rita*, a play written for and first performed by the Royal Shakespeare Company in 1980. Most people are familiar with the 1983 film version which, although it boasts fine performances by Michael Caine and Julie Walters, in my opinion dilutes the original text's powerful and hard-hitting dramatic force.

Rita is a young hairdresser who has become increasingly dissatisfied with her life. She enrols on an Open University literature course. Her tutor is Frank, a professor at the local university, whose excessive drinking betrays his own dissatisfaction with his life. Both are profoundly changed by the relationship which develops. We see how Rita experiments with different aspects of middle-class lifestyle before finally passing her exam. The play ends as she considers her various choices for the next stage of her life. Frank, meanwhile, is about to go on sabbatical after one too many drunken incidents. He too is beginning a new stage in his life.

The play is a two-hander, and is therefore intensely focused throughout. We hear of other characters – Rita's husband, father and mother, her flatmate Trish, Frank's girlfriend Julia, students with whom Rita is friendly, clients in the hairdressing salon where Rita works – and therefore gain a sense of the wider community, without ever feeling a dissipation of the strength of the developing relationship between Frank and Rita. This perspective is an unusual one for students, who are used to television drama with large casts and whose previous contact with drama is most likely to have been with Shakespeare. The choice made by the writer to restrict the cast to two characters is a fruitful line of discussion, particularly when exploring the dramatic qualities of the text which result from this choice.

The second aspect of the play which students find surprising, and sometimes difficult, is the set. Again, their familiarity with the myriad locations and naturalistic approach of television drama does not prepare them for a set which remains largely unchanged throughout the play. By considering the significance of the few small alterations to the set, students are able to see that a stage set has an importance which goes far beyond simply setting the scene. Rita's first exchange with Frank on the subject of the faulty door handle emphasizes his isolation and the danger of incarceration in his ivory tower: 'one of these days you'll be shouting "Come in" and it'll go on forever because the poor sod on the other side of the door won't be able to get in. An' you won't be able to get out.'

Rita is Frank's 'breath of air', his potential saviour from academic self-imprisonment, but Frank is an unwilling participant in his own redemption; later in the play he is appalled by her suggestion that they have their tutorial outside on the grass. Instead, Rita tries to open a window:

> *Rita*: (*struggling to open the window*) It won't bleedin' budge.
> *Frank*: I'm not surprised, my dear. It hasn't been opened in generations.
> *Rita*: (*abandoning it*) Tch. Y' need air in here, Frank. The room needs airing.
> *Frank*: This room does not need air, thank you very much.

The symbolism here is accessible to students because it is communicated not only through language but also through dramatic action.

In the same way that they can learn to read the characters' actions for meaning, the play also exemplifies for students how, whether we like it or not, language defines much more than just character. The cultural references used by Frank and Rita speak eloquently of their social class and educational experience. Frank's literary allusions are meaningless to Rita at the beginning of the play: to Rita, Yeats is a wine lodge. Her frame of reference is popular culture in a domestic setting: television, film, populist history, margarine. Frank is equally at sea with Charlie's Angels, Eliot Ness and Flora. Rita sums up their mutual incomprehension succinctly: 'You wouldn't watch ITV though, would y'? It's all BBC with you, isn't it?' The arguably outdated ITV/working-class, BBC/middle-class connection may need explaining to students, but it is a worthwhile digression into the early history of television. The whole discussion is a valuable way of exploring the different languages that co-exist in society: the languages of parents, teachers, the police, teenagers, each with their own frames of reference and cultural norms.

Linked closely with this is the way in which Russell has written Rita's speech to indicate a strong regional accent. A couple of references to local areas and football teams make it clear that Russell has set the play in Liverpool, but with only very minor changes it could be set anywhere. I like the idea of a Yorkshire Rita, a Scottish Rita or an Essex Rita. The point would be the same: that a regional accent is too often assumed to be a sign of inferior intelligence, lack of education and lower social status than an accent using Received Pronunciation and Standard English. I have found students to be noticeably prejudiced about accent and dialect, a state of mind which presumably arises from ignorance. There is ample opportunity here to develop into analysis of attitudes towards accent and dialect. (It is also a good opportunity to furnish them with more precise language in which to discuss accent, dialect and class. Many of my students persisted in referring to Rita as 'common' because of the way she spoke, ironically unaware that they shared both her colloquial rhythms of speech and, technically, her social class.) In Act II, Scene ii Rita experiments with Received Pronunciation, resulting in 'a peculiar voice', in response to a comment made by her new (middle-class) flatmate Trish: 'there is not a lot of point in discussing beautiful literature in an ugly voice.' Frank compares Rita's strained voice to that of a Dalek. His choice of comparison alerts us to the fact that while Rita's education is increasingly allowing her access into what she regards as a rarefied middle-class lifestyle, at the same time through his relationship with Rita, Frank is becoming more aware of the world around him.

As Rita's education develops, she begins to find that she increasingly inhabits a world halfway between her working-class origins and Frank's middle-class life. When invited to dinner at Frank's, she can't decide what to wear and doesn't know which wine to take, and is acutely conscious of her status as 'a half-caste'. In his article '*Oleanna* and *Educating Rita*' (*The English Review*, Vol. 9) Bernard O'Keeffe points out that Rita expresses this in terms of language: 'I'm a freak. I can't talk to the people I live with any more. An' I can't talk to the likes of them on Saturday or them out there ['proper' students] because I can't learn the language.' Once Rita has learned the language, her relationship with Frank deteriorates. She no longer needs him to guide her in 'what clothes to wear, what wine to buy, what plays to see, what papers and books to read, I can do without you.' At the same time Frank is horrified by her new intellectual confidence, and accuses her of using education as a means to an end: 'Have you come all this way for so very, very little?

... Found a culture, have you, Rita? Found a better song to sing, have you? No, you've found a different song, that's all – and on your lips it's shrill and hollow and tuneless.'

For me, one of the great strengths of the play is its refusal to present one social class and lifestyle as superior to another. Both working-class and middle-class life are closely examined and held up for criticism. It could be argued that Russell is in fact suggesting that there is no such thing as the working class and the middle class: that all that separates two groups of people is their educational experience. He is careful not to lay blame for a failed education purely on the educational system, but considers also the ways in which the working class could be accused of having colluded in their own educational underachievement. Rita disputes the very existence of working-class culture: 'I've read about it. I've never seen it though ... I just see everyone pissed, or on the Valium, tryin' to get from one day to the next.' She accuses the traditional working-class media and the unions of covering up 'the disease', and expresses her frustration at the low aspirations of her husband: 'He thinks we've got choice because we can go into a pub that sells eight different kinds of lager.' Most importantly, she articulates the significance of her schooling in the way her life has turned out so far:

> *Frank*: Rita, why didn't you ever become what you call a proper student?
> *Rita*: What? After goin' to the school I went to?

Russell is careful to acknowledge Rita's own responsibility for her failure at school, and places it within the context of community and peer pressure:

> *Rita*: See, if I'd started takin' school seriously I would have had to become different from me mates, and that's not allowed.
> *Frank*: By whom?
> *Rita*: By your mates, by your family, by everyone. So y'never admitted that school could be anything other than useless.

This is a hugely meaningful area to explore with students. Do they share the younger Rita's low expectations of herself? Do they feel, like Rita, that peer pressure and community expectation affects their attitude towards school? If so, how can this be overcome? Rita has had a second chance at education, but her success has come at the expense of alienating her husband and irreversibly changing her life. Asked about the ways in which the play had affected their thinking, one of my students wrote: 'It makes you think about what you are trying to do, and who you're doing it for.' Indeed.

The theme of class is one which students take very seriously. They certainly recognize it in this play. A year after studying *Educating Rita*, nearly all my students nominated class as a key aspect of the play. I think this reflects their interest in ideas about class, and perhaps also the fact that they are not exposed to explicit discussion about class in other areas of the curriculum. There seems to be no place for it in the PSHE curriculum, and their contact with manifestations of class in history lessons is likely to frame the subject in a very different context. Although it is an integral part of their lives, they rarely possess the language to express their opinions about it.

Finally, I would like to consider the ending of *Educating Rita*. When asked what they disliked about the play, many students nominated the ending. 'It didn't end with a definite answer . . .' wrote one student, with some feeling. For such students, the 'problem' is that there is no ending. Rita has passed her exam and is now in a position to decide what to do next: 'Because of what you'd given me, I had a choice . . . I might go to France. I might go to me mother's. I might even have a baby. I'll make a decision, I'll choose.'

The point here, of course, is that previously Rita's choices were made for her, and now she is in control. Rather than being an ending, it is a new beginning for Rita. Similarly, Frank is preparing for a new beginning. He has committed one too many drunken indiscretions and is packing up his books and moving on. He tells Rita he is going to Australia, but it is likely we are meant to read this metaphorically, as he has earlier referred to Australia as an apt place to send a 'convict' like himself. Whatever his destination, it is clear that for the first time in many years Frank is leaving the security of his room and venturing into a life elsewhere. He seems apprehensive about his ability to cope alone – he asks Rita to join him, without ever really thinking that she will – and we find ourselves wondering about what the future can really be for Frank. It is at this point in the play that the difference in the two characters' attitudes towards education is at its most striking. For Rita, education has been a means to an end. By educating herself, Rita has found access to a new way of living. As Bernard O'Keeffe points out, Rita has found a new language, and in that language an enabling power. For Frank, on the other hand, education is a way of life in itself. His teaching is conducted in witty, sarcastic discourse which often lacks true substance beneath its polished veneer. Of the two characters at the end of the play, Frank is the one who seems to be lacking the knowledge to succeed in a new life. It seems all too likely that he will simply unpack his books in a different room, unscrew a new bottle of whisky and set about re-creating his former life.

* * *

With its complex themes and lack of resolution, *Educating Rita* in my experience works best with the middle to upper ability range. Another of Russell's plays, which deals with some of the same issues in a more direct and accessible way, is particularly suitable for studying with lower ability students. In my experience it has never failed: the well-observed characterization, uncompromising use of the teenage verna-cular and straightforward narrative line all appeal to even the most hardened self-proclaimed hater of literature, as does the opportunity to get involved by taking either a large or small but still significant role in a class reading. *Our Day Out* deals with the experiences of the 'Progress Class', a group of students struggling to read and write, on a day trip away from their school in inner-city Liverpool. The day is led by Mrs Kay, the teacher of the Progress Class, and two like-minded younger teachers, but at the last minute they are joined by Mr Briggs, a representative of the Headmaster sent to maintain order and discipline. During the course of the day the different educational philosophies held by Briggs and Mrs Kay are revealed, and ultimately force them into direct confrontation. A recognizable cast of pupils provide comedy and pathos which never slips into sentimentality. Originally a television play (available on video from the BBC), the screenplay format is an excellent way into modern drama for less able students. Their familiarity and ease with television helps to break down barriers of prejudice and reluc-tance, especially when it comes to reading aloud. Typecasting is eminently possible, with the energy of boisterous male students particularly effectively channelled into the reading of characters Digga and Reilly.

The accuracy of Russell's characterization in this play is clearly a result of his own teaching experience at Shorefields Comprehensive School. Indeed, we are told in the Preface to the Heinemann edition of the play that Russell participated in a school trip with many common ingredients to that in *Our Day Out*. The creation of art from real experience is a concept which is well worth broaching with students, albeit in a simplistic way: would Russell have based his characters directly on those he knew? Would he be likely to keep incidents the same, or change them? Why? The film *Shakespeare in Love*, which depicts Shakespeare creating *Romeo and Juliet* out of the fabric of his own love life, can be a useful point of comparison. Students are, after all, quite familiar with the concept of recasting events in a more 'creative' light!

There are ten main pupil characters, and as Russell develops them in more detail during the first section of the play, we are given glimpses of the backgrounds and upbringings which have affected their develop-ment. One character, Andrews, is addicted to nicotine and says he has been smoking since he was 8. Briggs asks him what his parents say about it:

> *Andrews*: Sir, sir, me mum says nott'n about it but when me dad comes home, sir, sir, he belts me.
> *Briggs*: Because you smoke?
> *Andrews*: Sir, no sir, because I won't give him one.

Throughout the play Briggs is the representative of the educated middle classes. Well-meaning, committed to the belief that education breeds opportunity, he is naive and ignorant concerning the reality of the current and future lives of the pupils. Andrews' account of his parents' relationship leaves Briggs speechless:

> *Briggs*: Your father goes to sea, does he?
> *Andrews*: What? No, sir.
> *Briggs*: You said 'when he comes home', I thought you meant he was away a lot.
> *Andrews*: He is sir, but he doesn't go to sea.
> *Briggs*: What does he do?
> *Andrews*: I dunno sir, sir, he just comes round every now and then an' has a barney with me mam. Then he goes off again. I think he tries to get money off her but she won't give it him though. She hates him. We all hate him.
> *(Pause.)*

The widely differing perspectives of the pupils and Briggs are well illustrated early on in the play when the coach passes the Liverpool docks. Briggs points them out to Reilly:

> *Briggs*: Can't you see? Look, those buildings. Don't you ever bother looking at what's around you?
> *Reilly*: It's only the docks, sir.
> *Briggs*: You don't get buildings like that any more. Just look at the work that must have gone into that.
> *Reilly*: Do you like it down here, sir?
> *Briggs*: I'm often down here at weekends, taking notes, photographs...
> *Reilly*: Me old man works down here, sir.
> *Briggs*: What does he think about it?
> *Reilly*: He hates it.
> *Briggs*: His job or the place?
> *Reilly*: The whole lot.

For Briggs the docks are a wealth of interesting local history, while for Reilly and his father they represent a job to be hated – a job for which

Reilly, who is in his last year at school, may well be next in line. But Russell is not asking for unqualified sympathy for Reilly, rather for our recognition of the limitations of his world and for exploration of the factors which have led to it.

At the core of the play is the clash of two conflicting educational ideologies embodied in the views held by Briggs and Mrs Kay. They sum up the tension between a progressive, child-centred education and a traditional disciplinarian approach. At first this is articulated with a humorous spin: Mr Briggs is horrified when Mrs Kay does not make the children line up before entering a café, for example. But after an incident at a zoo in which several animals are temporarily liberated from their compounds by the children, Briggs expresses his anger to them:

> Is it any wonder that people won't do anything for you? The minute we start to treat you as real people, what happens? ... you act like animals, animals! Well, I've learned a lesson today. Oh, yes I have. I've learned that trust is something you people don't understand. Now, I'm warning you, all of you, don't expect any more trust from me!

The abuse of trust that Briggs feels so strongly is an interesting issue to explore with students, particularly from their own perspective. There is plenty of evidence in the play that Russell means us to recognize that there is little reason for the pupils themselves to trust anyone, least of all society, to provide a decent job and life free from poverty and danger. While the children run wild among the ruins of Conwy Castle, Briggs confronts Mrs Kay: 'You are on their side, aren't you?' She points out that 'Most of them were rejects on the day they were born ... even if you cared, do you think you could educate these kids, my remedial kids? Because you're a fool if you do. You won't educate them because nobody wants them educating.' Briggs is genuinely shocked and offended by Mrs Kay's pragmatic and seemingly defeatist attitude about the prospects of her pupils. Her starkly expressed understanding of the education system is that 'you won't teach them because you're in a job that's designed and funded to fail.' This overtly political reading of the state school system might well seem as applicable now as it did over twenty years ago when the play was first written. It can certainly seem all too true to students sitting in poorly maintained classrooms, sharing texts and providing their own writing paper. But it is important to recognize that, typically for Russell, Mrs Kay's is not the only point of view expressed in the play. While students do not warm to Briggs because of his authoritarian style and lack of respect for individual pupils, his deeply held belief that education creates opportunity is one with which they are more comfortable than Mrs Kay's uncompromising political views. In the dramatic climax of the play, Briggs finds himself alone on a cliff-top with Carol, one of the youngest and most vulnerable of the children. She tells him she doesn't want to return to Liverpool; she wants to 'stay here. Where it's nice.' Briggs tries ordering her down, then cajoling, and finally talks to her about the possibilities of realizing her dream of living by the sea: 'what's to stop you working hard at school from now on, getting a good job and then moving out here when you're old enough? Eh?' His articulation of everything he believes about education – and one senses that as soon as he says it, he can hear how unconvincing it sounds – is powerfully and painfully undercut by Carol's response: 'Don't be so friggin' stupid.' Carol may not believe that education can change her life for the better, but she does at least still believe in relationships. Briggs finally persuades her down from the cliff by smiling at her and talking to her gently. A key discussion point for students is to consider which teacher they would prefer to have teaching them, and why. Their choice reveals much about their attitudes towards education and their expectations of themselves. It is a different route into the same question posed in *Educating Rita*: what is education for, and what do you want from it?

The success of this text in the classroom and its very great value for study with students are due to a variety of factors: the strong and accurate characterization, the clear episodic narrative structure and the realistic use of the teenage vernacular. Perhaps the most significant factor is the comedy of the play. It seems to me the mark of a true classic for a text to address such essentially serious concerns alongside such well-observed humour. The issue of social class is again important, and the very different vocabulary, accent and dialect of the teachers and their students are a good way into this. Teachers reading and discussing this text with a class will very probably succeed in enabling students, perhaps for the first time, to conduct real dialogue with their teacher about ideas, relationships and literature, and may well find that their relationship with the class is permanently enhanced as a result.

Finally, I would like to examine a third Willy Russell play, one which I have taught as part of the Wide Reading coursework assignment required by NEAB. The play is *Terraces*. It was originally written in 1993 for the BBC's 'Scene' strand and the script is still available free of charge from the BBC Education Department. The play is still shown regularly during the 'Scene' season. I teach the play alongside the short story 'The Sexton's Hero' by Elizabeth Gaskell, in which similar themes are treated very differently.

Terraces is set, unsurprisingly, on a terraced street in an inner-city area. The action takes place over a seven-day period. The play opens with a joyful scene in the local pub where the community is celebrating the success of its football team, which has won through to the Cup Final. A chance remark made by one of the locals, Danny, gives his friends and neighbours the idea of painting their houses yellow, the team's colour, in order to show their support. They all carry it out with enthusiasm, except Danny. As days go by, more and more pressure is exerted on him and his family to conform. His wife and son, humiliated by their friends, leave him to try to force him to comply. Finally he is held prisoner in his own home by his friends while the house is painted. As they finish and contemplate the uniform colour of the street with satisfaction, Danny emerges from his house with a bag and walks away. The credits roll, while ironic football chants of 'We're United' ring out on the soundtrack. The ongoing football metaphor makes the play particularly attractive to boys, and they are often able to articulate highly successfully the significance of football to a community and its relevance as a metaphor in the play.

The play has plenty in it worthy of close study. The dominant theme of conformity is easily accessible and relevant to students, especially in the context of peer pressure depicted in the play. Russell uses some clever touches early on in the play to introduce this theme. His son, trying to complete a crossword puzzle, asks him to solve the clues 'Hysterical gang ... three letters' and 'ten-letter word that means "one who always agrees"'. Danny supplies 'mob' for the first, but leaves the second to us. As the situation deepens, we see that 'community spirit', as Danny's wife calls it, can develop into something much more sinister. First the wishes of the individual are ignored: 'What do you mean, you don't want to? You know it's not up to you. The street's decided.' Later he becomes a pariah, shunned as a potentially subversive presence. Eddie, the unofficial community leader, tells him: 'You're a case, you are, Danny. Always were a bit of the awkward one. A bit different ... an awkward bugger.'

Russell skilfully shows Eddie's development from a charismatic pub regular, described as 'a laugh' in an early scene by Danny's wife Susan, into an intimidating and threatening figure. On the third day he warns Danny: 'You'd better bleedin' well grow up. Or you'll be sorry.' On the fourth day, in front of a group of neighbours, he shouts at Danny: 'You need treatment you do ... You're soft in the head, son.' Later that same day in the pub he gives a rabble-rousing speech in which he declares:

> This country is ruled by majorities ... It's him and his sort that give this country a bad name, who'd drag it down into the slime of the sewer if they were given half a chance. We've got a marvellous opportunity here; an opportunity to show the world the hard work and pride of this community. And to allow one headcase to deny us that opportunity would be a crime.

Finally, having achieved his objective by force, Eddie tells Danny that 'when this is over, we can all go back to normal. There'll be a drink waiting for you in the pub.' Through the character of Eddie, students can explore the mindset and working methods of a bully. By looking at the street as a microcosm of society, they can also consider the relationship between the domestic and the political, and the potential for intolerance and fascism. The problematic area of the relationship between the individual and society is addressed without resolution, because the ending of the play, like that of both *Educating Rita* and *Our Day Out*, is not really an ending at all. It seems to show the outcast leaving the community which has rejected and held up to ridicule his individual wishes, but with further thought the audience/reader is likely to challenge their first reading. Surely Danny, depicted throughout the play as a loving father and husband, would not simply walk away from his family for good? The reader/audience knows there is more to this situation, and can only speculate on the outcome.

For students, the issues of peer pressure, bullying, and the desirability or otherwise of achieving conformity are particularly resonant. They are able to make explicit links between the thematic concerns of the play and their own lives. One student commented: 'I've learned to stand up to people if they gang up because I'm different.' Another wrote: 'It [the play] showed me how you can be independent and you don't have to follow groups or do what you're told.' The character of Eddie in particular generated a lot of discussion and much recognition. It is also important to recognize and discuss the depiction of women in the play, who are shown to be particularly influenced by community opinion and keen not to be seen as different in any way. Danny's wife even colludes in his ultimate humiliation, tricking him into opening the door to his friends, who then hold him prisoner while the house is painted. (This is an especially fruitful area of comparison with 'The Sexton's Hero'.) Students' reactions to Danny and his actions are wide-ranging and deeply felt, with all students ultimately recognizing that the situation is an impossible one which has no straightforward solution or easy compromise. It is all too easy for students to find comparable situations both in their own lives and in wider current affairs.

It is this lack of explicit moralizing in Russell's plays which, for me, makes them such powerful and effective teaching material. Each of the texts I have discussed raises many more questions than it answers, forcing students to develop their own thinking and ideas in order to make coherent meaning from the text. The GCSE assessment criteria use the word 'think' far too little in my opinion, and we are doing our students a disservice if we do not encourage them through our choice of texts to extend the boundaries of their thinking. (This is particularly important when we consider how we expect them to be fully active thinkers at A level.) Reading and discussing Russell's plays involves broaching a very adult world of uncertainty; a world in which there are many questions and few answers. When they read and explore these plays, students are thinking not just about literature, and about created characters, situations and language, but also about themselves: about their position in society, their expectations of themselves and their attitudes towards education. They are developing not only as GCSE English and English literature students, but also as young people.

ACKNOWLEDGEMENTS

With thanks to my students Philip Clarke, Adam Coope, Jennifer Stradling and Annette Wren for their quotations.

Part III

Teaching Literature Post-16

Chapter 7

Readings and Representations in *The Strange Case of Dr Jekyll and Mr Hyde*

James Hansford

Note: Page references are to the Penguin Popular Classics edition (London, 1994)

Like Conrad's *Heart of Darkness* (1902), Stevenson's *The Strange Case of Dr Jekyll and Mr Hyde* (1886) can lay claim to being a classic text for students embarking on advanced study of literature, whether in the sixth form or at undergraduate level. By 'classic' I mean merely exemplary for an examination of reading and representation, for a study of the mechanisms, practices, possibilities – and impossibilities – offered by narrative which Stevenson's story, no less than Conrad's, so insistently foregrounds. That both of these texts lie within the range of late Victorian, *fin-de-siècle* and early Modernist writing, within the emergent intellectual sphere populated, if not popularized by the ideas and influence of Marx, Nietzsche, Darwin and Freud is of interest and significance, though of less immediate concern than it might be within the contexts set out here.

Stevenson's story is short but, like the 'dwarf' (p. 52) Hyde, it obscures a greater mass of startling complexity, a resonant textual body out of all proportion to its brief compass. The contexts I want to examine here are ones which have certainly exercised critics in recent years, whether narratological, psychoanalytical or deconstructionist, and which engage with the story's richness and ambivalence, its doubleness and obscurities. These contexts and considerations can challenge assumptions and readily held convictions regarding both textuality and reality. They can confront students with problems of understanding and evaluation and allow them a greater self-conscious-ness about their own critical practice. Right at the outset of A-Level study, several weeks' examination of Stevenson's story can refashion students' critical practice, implicitly rather than explicitly introducing them to literary theories upon which teachers may wish to consolidate; in any event, questions as to how narrative is shaped, reality fashioned into text, reading governed by assumptions and priorities can be addressed fully and fairly with Stevenson's story as the exemplar text.

The Strange Case of Dr Jekyll and Mr Hyde is a 'classic' text for the examination of literary representation on a number of grounds. By reason of its obsessive concern with duplicity, it reveals the fluidity of 'character', the indeterminacy of 'self'; an interrogation of what is meant by 'good' and 'evil' (so often thought of as 'given') obliges students to reconsider these terms and the characters who deploy and invite them. Duplicity likewise compels consideration of text and subtext, that which is shown and that which is hidden. The story's multiple narrators and its use of Utterson as focalizer prompt investigation of what, long ago, was termed 'point of view', while Stevenson's treatment of 'story' and 'plot' invites detailed study of the text's construction. Meanwhile, its careful delineation of geography, understood as both fictional and textual space, compels any reader to attend to tropes and figures. Readings focusing upon gender and class bring to light the 'political unconscious', and also the larger questions of the 'unconscious', whether as a way of structuring the relations between 'characters' or, further, as a means of apprehending the reading process upon which characters and oneself as reader are engaged. Finally, representation itself is at stake in this story in which naming and narration, writing and textuality, expose the limits of what can be shown in narrative.

'HE, I SAY – I CANNOT SAY, I' (p. 84)

Dr Jekyll strikes the keynote of his story when he remarks that 'all human beings, as we meet them, are commingled out of good and evil' (p. 73). The details, too familiar to rehearse, explore the manner in which the 'fortress of identity' (p. 71) is shaken and how a 'profound duplicity of life' (p. 69) develops and destroys him. What I have called the 'fluidity of character' challenges habits of thought which regard personality as both fixed and readily defined. It shows itself not merely in the division of personality between Dr Jekyll and Mr Hyde (Dr Jekyll himself misleadingly refers to the former as his 'original and better self' (p. 79)) but, most importantly, in the 'composite' (p. 79) nature of Dr Jekyll. This is the 'old Henry Jekyll, that incongruous compound' (p. 74), 'better' (p. 79) only in degree, and 'original' (p. 79) only in the trivial sense of antedating what Nabokov refers to as the 'hybridization' process. Jekyll is 'original' (p. 79) only in the sense that circumstances in this story can be referred to as 'singular' (pp. 38, 72) (and it is Hyde, not Jekyll, who is referred to, also misleadingly, as 'single' (p. 73)) and is no less ironic than Jekyll's claim to be able to see his life 'as a whole' (p. 81) at precisely the point at which it is manifestly falling apart. How 'full', one asks students to consider, is Dr Jekyll's 'statement' if identity is 'compound' and never fully present to the autobiographer?

'If Edward Hyde', the essay question runs, 'is "pure evil" ' (p. 73), then who or what is Henry Jekyll? Hyde is 'express and single' (p. 73) Jekyll claims, while Jekyll himself has an 'imperfect and divided countenance' (p. 73). The opposition suggested *between* Jekyll and Hyde is, of course, an opposition *within* Jekyll, the 'incongruous compound' (p. 74). Stevenson's use of the word 'compound' is telling: Jekyll, one might say, is precisely the 'unknown impurity' (p. 87) which permits metamorphosis. Jekyll's discovery, as he relates it, may indeed be 'singular' (in the sense discussed above) but it is also 'profound' (p. 72), an assonantal 'compound(ing)' of 'elements' (p. 72) to reveal more markedly than before, to appropriate Nabokov's expression, the *hybridization* of Henry Jekyll.

Students ought also to tackle Hyde's own far from 'singular' (p. 72) nature, because he also operates in a 'compound' (p. 74) fashion. For all that he is 'pure evil' (p. 73) (whatever that may be thought to mean), he remains yoked to Jekyll who 'now with the most sensitive apprehensions, now with a greedy gusto, projected and shared in the pleasures and adventures of Hyde' (p. 79). In a familial, even perhaps Oedipal language to which we shall return, Jekyll relates that although Hyde had 'more than a son's indifference', Jekyll had 'more than a father's interest' (p. 79). Further, in figures which compound familial, physiognomical and birth images, Hyde is said to be 'closer than a wife, closer than an eye' (p. 86) (and, one might add, an 'I'). Jekyll 'felt it struggle to be born' (p. 86). Jekyll and Hyde are, at this point, umbilically connected.

That the struggle between characters is one within character itself allows one to consider afresh the provenance of Hyde from the 'irregularities' Jekyll asserts he 'hid ... with an almost morbid sense of shame' (p. 69). Jekyll's 'original' (p. 79) self is a duplicitous, therefore hybrid one, an 'honourable and distinguished' manner tinctured with a 'certain impatient gaiety of disposition' (p. 69). 'License' (p. 82), one should insist, exists not *despite* but *because of* propriety: it is precisely more because of the 'exacting nature of my aspirations, than any particular degradation in my faults, that made me what I was' (p. 69). Far from validating, as careless readers might suppose, the high-minded, genteel Victorian professionalism of which Dr Jekyll is so signal an example, Stevenson is interrogating precisely those values and what they too carefully obscure. And duplicity is not confined to the compound Dr Jekyll. Students ought also to consider the role of subsidiary characters who can so often seem peripheral, and the patterns they create, confirm or confound; it is worth observing the ways in which other figures in the story – Utterson, Enfield, the interestingly termed 'hide-bound pedant' (p. 27) Dr Lanyon and a host of other characters – themselves more or less representative of the world of respectable sobriety which Stevenson constructs, are opened out through this approach.

Bachelorhood pervades this world, a world of lawyers and doctors, of austerity and propriety, of 'sombre spirits' and 'dry divinity' (p. 17). One is struck by the undue prominence accorded to Mr Utterson (for all but the closing two chapters, the story's focalizer), to Dr Lanyon, Mr Enfield and Poole among others. What is equally striking is that it is not just what Hyde says or does which is of interest, but also the *effect* he exerts on those with whom he comes into contact. As Jekyll points out in his statement, 'none would come near to me at first without a visible misgiving of the flesh' (p. 73). If he erupts, like Nabokov's 'precipitate', from Dr Jekyll, he irrupts upon other characters with startling consequences: 'one look', records Enfield, 'brought out the sweat on me like running' (p. 12); Sawbones, as he is termed, the 'usual cut-and-dry apothecary, of no particular age and colour, with a strong Edinburgh accent, and about as emotional as a bagpipe' (p. 12), is transformed by contact with Hyde: 'every time he looked ... [he] turned sick and white with the desire to kill him' (p. 12); further confining illustration to the opening chapter, the women, a 'circle of hateful faces' were 'as wild as harpies' (p. 12). The examples of such turns of temperament, of the hidden temper of such customarily reserved, proper and genteel figures, are legion. Students, when asked on a 'blind tasting' exercise in class in the course of a discussion of this trait, which character speaks thus ' "Hold your tongue" ... with a ferocity of accent' (p. 49), confidently answer that it is Hyde. They are astonished to discover that it is Jekyll's otherwise 'well-dressed, elderly servant' (p. 24) Poole, addressing, what is more, a weeping maid. She is the housemaid who on 'The Last Night' (from which this example comes) 'broke into hysterical whimpering' at 'the sight of Mr Utterson' (p. 49). A good deal is 'broken', incidentally, in this text – silence, voices, sticks, keys, bonds, bounds and packets. Gender considerations aside, one should none the less pause at the account of Mr Hyde's landlady: her 'evil face' was 'smoothed by hypocrisy' and (the text reads 'but') 'her manners were excellent'; her 'flash of odious joy' (p. 32) is not unrelated to the police officer's response, recounted shortly before, when the identity of Hyde's latest victim, Sir Danvers Carew, is revealed: 'his eye lighted up with professional ambition' (p. 31). Furthermore, it is not difficult to relate these

images of light and fire to the 'great flame of anger' (p. 30) which erupts
in Hyde, to the 'something eminently human [which] beaconed from
[Utterson's] eye' (p. 9), to the 'scroll of lighted pictures' (p. 20) Utterson
views when reviewing Enfield's account of Hyde's encounter with the
young girl. It is not that light and dark – literally and figuratively – are not
deployed conventionally here. But if Jekyll hides rather than 'blazon[s]'
his 'irregularities' (p. 69), it would be to lighten the darkness were he to
do otherwise, to do what Marlow's tales in Conrad's *Heart of Darkness*
are said to do, to make the darkness visible. The lamplit street Enfield
recalls in the opening chapter is one in which 'a man listens and listens
and begins to long for the sight of a policeman' (p. 11). The lamps in
Soho encountered *en route* to Hyde's lodgings 'had never been
extinguished or had been kindled afresh to combat this mournful
reinvasion of darkness' which seemed 'in the lawyer's eyes, like a
district of some city in a nightmare' (pp. 31–2). Utterson feels tainted
with criminality when he becomes 'conscious of some touch of that
terror of the law and the law's officers which may at times assail the
most honest' (p. 32), an effect which seems to turn 'inside out' (p. 33)
(as Hyde's pockets are, in the room he shortly afterwards searches)
Utterson's customary identity.

From how Hyde affects, infects or rather catalyses to what affects
Hyde is to consider what is thought to break or breach the bounds of
permitted behaviour, whatever lies enwombed in Dr Jekyll. Bearing the
'stamp' of Jekyll's 'lower elements' (p. 71), Hyde is one of the 'polar
twins' struggling in the 'agonized womb of consciousness' (p. 71) to be
born. As Dr Jekyll's 'more upright twin' (p. 70) can be said to produce
the 'doubled up' (p. 53) figure of Hyde, the latter a consequence of the
former, neither of them strictly speaking 'original' (p. 79), so Hyde is
revealed as the surplus energy generated by 'restraint' (p. 70) and not to
be unproblematically consigned as 'evil'. '*If* Hyde is pure evil ...' one
asks students to consider, and trusts they will worry about – and worry
away – at both those terms. After all, Jekyll points out that Hyde appears
'natural and human ... bore a livelier image of the spirit' (p. 73) than the
one which maintained an image of 'effort, virtue and control' and which
is the 'imperfect countenance' (p. 73) of Dr Jekyll. 'His love of life',
Jekyll marvels, 'is wonderful' (p. 87). That Jekyll can also remark that the
'child of Hell had nothing human' (p. 84) only serves to demonstrate
that accounts of Hyde in the text are necessarily tinged or tainted by a
consciousness tempered by the 'restrictions of natural life' (p. 81). Hyde
is Jekyll's Hyde as Jekyll is Hyde's Jekyll.

Students are quick to notice the language of diabolism ('Satan's
signature' (p. 23)) which so often characterizes descriptions of Hyde,
from Utterson, Enfield, Dr Lanyon and others, as well as from Dr Jekyll.

As easily noted is the language of bestiality, with references to Dr Fell, to Hyde's 'ape-like fury' (p. 30), to how he 'snarled aloud into a savage laugh' (p. 23) and behaved with 'bestial avidity' (p. 76). Moreover, there is 'something troglodytic' (p. 23) about him, Utterson supposes. But students need to be directed beyond these crude descriptions to what, for example, we are explicitly told is Hyde's devotion to 'self' (p. 76) and to what might be understood by his 'good pleasure', however 'malign and villainous' (p. 76) the narrator of the closing 'Full Statement' asserts it to be.

Wishing to generate productive confusion rather than effect a crude reversal of moral valuation here, one finds it difficult to whole-heartedly condemn the impulses which propel Hyde into action or to view with disapprobation, any more than does Dr Jekyll, the 'solution of the bonds of obligation' (p. 83). Sadism, cruelty, murder and abuse are arguably, in Stevenson's story, perversions and developments of the sex drive. One of the many hidden representations in Stevenson's 'strange case' is precisely the sexual life and one of the telling obscurities concerns the otherness of women, Dr Jekyll's veiled admission of the sexual life, of the 'current of disordered sensual images running like a mill race in [his] fancy' (p. 72) (one of many water images of (dis)solution in the story). The location of Hyde's apartment in the salubrious area of Soho is a telling detail, as is reference to its 'slatternly passengers' (p. 31), to the 'many women' (p. 32) who inhabit it; the scene recalls that with which the story opens, a location in which 'shop fronts stood along that thoroughfare with an air of invitation, like rows of smiling saleswomen' (p. 10). One should recall here the Jekyll/Hyde symbiosis in terms of husband and 'wife' (p. 86) and note Poole's description of Hyde's weeping on 'The Last Night', 'like a woman or a lost soul', and so affectively that Poole asserts 'I could have wept too' (p. 55) (as Jekyll can feel 'pity' (p. 87) for Hyde).

There are many respects, therefore, in which Hyde assumes the 'otherness' of Dr Jekyll, as he does, in lesser measure, others in the bachelor society which Stevenson represents. It is a society for whom women are the repressed, feared 'other' and as intoxicating as wine. Hyde is said to 'drink ... pleasure' (p. 76), but less abstemiously, one must conclude, than Utterson and his 'Guest' (*sic*). They sit precisely either side of the hearth while, strategically placed 'midway between at a nicely calculated distance from the fire, a bottle of a particular old wine' (p. 37) awaits them. Under its influence 'the lawyer melted' within the bounds of permitted intoxication for 'the acids were long ago resolved' (p. 37). The contrast with Hyde's figurative intoxication and with Jekyll's literal but analogical ingestion is inescapable.

Character is indeed fluid in Stevenson's story, neither fixed nor readily defined. Like the 'situation' Dr Jekyll writes of to Utterson, character is essentially 'nameless' (p. 59), something 'I cannot name' (p. 42), as Jekyll's own, at one point, is one that Enfield 'can't mention' (p. 13). 'He, I say – I cannot say, I' (p. 84). Character is energy and impulse, formation and restraint, the otherness of self, 'a mere polity of multifarious, incongruous and independent denizens' (p. 70). Students are warily intrigued by the suggestiveness of names and naming in Stevenson's story. Utterson's own sobriquet 'Mr Seek' in relation to 'Mr Hyde' (p. 21) is straightforward and resonant enough, but what of Dr Jekyll? It has been suggested that the *y e* in Hyde mirrors the *e y* in Jekyll (as one's handwriting mirrors the other's), that Jekyll is the 'I' the 'je' that *kills* the inner 'he': 'He, I say – I cannot say, I' (p. 84). On the Last Night, Utterson knew that he was looking on the body of a 'self-destroyer' (p. 56), one until then prey only to 'temporary suicide' (p. 86).

'STORY OF THE DOOR'

'Story of the Door' is the story with which the book begins. 'The reader is surely struck', one critic of the story has observed, 'by the extent to which the story is overrun by its narration, the latter strangely present as what the story is about.' This formulation should alert students to a number of considerations: there is, first and foremost, the issue of 'point of view', of who narrates; second, there is the relation between story and discourse, between the narrated events and their order of narration; and finally, there is the issue of narration as such, that which is 'strangely present as what the story is about'.

The third-person narration which governs the first eight chapters – the largest proportion of the story – does much to highlight, by contrast, the confessional nature of 'Henry Jekyll's Full Statement of the Case' and 'Dr Lanyon's Narrative' which precede it. Broadly speaking, the more or less abrupt transition can be figured as a movement from the outside to the inside, from what can be shown to what has, until a certain point, been hidden. The movement is an uneven one, however: conspicuously, there is Henry Jekyll's letter to Utterson, reproduced within the pages of 'The Last Night', his letter to Dr Lanyon recorded in the pages of the latter's narrative and any number of micro-narratives contained within the third-person accounts in the chapters in question. These are prompted by Stevenson's use of the 'austere' (p. 9) Mr Utterson as the story's focalizer, as 'Mr Seek' (p. 21) in pursuit of Mr Hyde who not only has his own experience to impart and his own thoughts to relate (as in the closing paragraph of 'Search for Mr Hyde') but encounters others who have theirs (Mr Enfield's 'Story of the Door' in Chapter 1, Poole's account of sighting Mr Hyde in 'The Last Night'). To whom, however, the maidservant in 'The Carew Murder Case' can be said to have 'narrated that experience' (p. 29) is far from clear but it offers yet another focalized narrative, here from a character 'romantically given' for whom, in her 'dream of musing' (p. 29), the act of 'insensate cruelty' (p. 30) she witnesses erupts from some hidden well of the unconscious.

Although Mr Utterson can be revealed as complicit with the drama he investigates and which Stevenson reports, students not unreasonably view him as the reader's delegate, an accessible link with readers who share a 'similar catholicity of good nature' (p. 9). The lawyer's name – and this is the first of many suggestions – is telling, for to 'utter' or to 'outer' is precisely Utterson's imperfectly realized function. It is also, of course, Lanyon's and Jekyll's in their respective accounts at the tale's close; and Utterson's own acquaintance with Mr Enfield, with whom a 'bond' (p. 10) is said to exist, with Dr Jekyll and Dr Lanyon ('inseparable friends' (p. 41)), with Guest and with Poole, either permits them to speak out or to elicit disclosure from Utterson himself: 'there was', for example, 'no man from whom (Utterson) kept fewer secrets than Mr Guest' (p. 37). Mr Utterson is a reader, a seeker, a speaker; he is both focalizer and narratee.

Stevenson's story is a complex relay of narratives, each enclosed within another as 'The Story of the Door' is the story with which the story begins. Within the narrative, letters, wills and documents are themselves enclosed within packets, drawers and safes. This fore-grounding of narrative as provisional and often mediated utterance replicates the uneasy relation between secrecy and disclosure in the narratives themselves and in the narrators and narratees who impart and absorb them. Indeed, it is difficult to distinguish narrators from narratees in a story in which frames themselves become part of some larger picture. Jekyll, for example, records that Hyde was 'scrawling in my own hand blasphemies on the pages of my books' (p. 87), such marginalia framing the printed page, reconfiguring the status and value of what it promotes.

If, however, Stevenson's story may be regarded as itself a hybrid construction, students again not unreasonably make claims for the authenticity of the story's final chapters. And if 'Dr Lanyon's Narrative' is but a covering letter, shall we say, for Henry Jekyll's 'Full Statement', Jekyll's account may be read as an utterance of what has been, up until now, more or less hidden from view. However, the chapter headings themselves, like all the others which cast experience into stories, incidents and cases, draw attention to partial, provisional versions of events, albeit Lanyon's revelations are remarkable and Jekyll's statement revelatory. The 'hide-bound' (p. 26) Lanyon is obliged to face the 'scientific heresies' (p. 27) from which he had recoiled, and he himself notes the 'odd, subjective disturbance caused by [Hyde's] neighbour-hood'. 'I set it down', he writes, 'to some idiosyncratic, personal distaste . . . but I have since had reason to believe the cause to lie much deeper in the nature of man, and to turn on some nobler hinge than the principle of hatred' (p. 65). This effect is of a piece with the others recorded. What is especially interesting in Lanyon's account is its residual reticence and its equation of knowledge with death – as it is in the stories of Poe ('The Masque of the Red Death'), Hawthorne ('The Birthmark') and George Eliot ('The Lifted Veil'). Lanyon's reticence is shown in an inability to 'set on paper' (p. 68) all that has passed and an inability to remain less than 'incredulous'. 'I ask myself if I believe it, and I cannot answer' (p. 68). And while the figure reverts to the identity of Jekyll 'like a man restored from death', his witness 'feels that [his] days are numbered, and that [he] must die' (p. 68). Dr Lanyon's narrative gestures beyond narrative.

As, indeed, does Henry Jekyll's 'Statement'. For all the statement closes with the word 'end', it is precisely Jekyll's continuance beyond narrative that the closing statement of his statement makes apparent. If Lanyon saw a 'man restored from death' (p. 68) only then to signal his own demise, Jekyll writes of a man signalling his (own) death beyond his own narrative.

Moreover, Jekyll's 'statement' is not, as we might say, fully enclosed. There is no return in Stevenson's text to the reading situation in which Utterson is engaged. It is as though the text, when closed, is most open to further scrutiny, and when open, most closed or enclosed upon the mysteries it cannot relate. Jekyll's letter, inserted within Lanyon's narrative, refers foolhardily to a resolution of all difficulties when 'my troubles will roll away like a story that is told' (p. 62). It is not to be. 'Henry Jekyll's Full Statement of the Case' is far from being the full story. And it is far from being simply Henry Jekyll's, one might suggest, when one considers the 'compound' nature of his identity, both 'He' and 'I'. Not only is there the question as to how 'full' is Dr Jekyll's 'statement', but also one as to how far it is even Dr Jekyll's when his identity is so involved with Hyde's, if not 'hide-bound' (p. 26) as Dr Lanyon is said to be. The story insistently suggests not only that the written medium is our only access to 'reality' but that, on several occasions within it, it is an unreliable medium through which to reach and ascertain the identity of the writer.

The question of narrative order, of the relation between story and discourse, is a necessary topic to address with students when consider-ing Stevenson's narrative before the transition to first-person address in its closing chapters. Put simply, why is there a discrepancy between the narrated events and their order of narration? The questions and mysteries which the story proposes are, of course, precisely because of the deferral of those closing accounts and because the opening eight chapters conceal and reveal, in so labyrinthine a fashion, the story to be told. The story is both overrun and occluded by its narration. It 'utters on' but in so 'broken' a fashion as to excite the reader and only partly to satisfy his search for knowledge. That 'The Last Night' should be the antepenultimate chapter suggests we should consider the rest addenda to the story, narration outrunning it, for narration seems here to be in excess of what it can plausibly and comprehensively narrate. Once more, the visible frames of narrative recontextualize the material, with Jekyll's final words writing the frame to direct us beyond it. How Utterson responds to them we are not told. He has moved from the position of surrogate reader – but a character all the same – to the position we, as readers, occupy.

'But what matters hand of write?' exclaims Poole on the last night. 'I've seen him' (p. 52). The privileging of sight over script has a long and complex history. The undecidability of the latter has often been set against the powerful truth of the former and of the revelations accessible in, as well as through the eye. Stevenson questions this opposition, not simply by making Hyde's appearance – what Poole sees – difficult to confirm ('the few who could describe him differed widely' (p. 33), there was a 'haunting sense of unexpressed deformity ... deformity without any namable malformation' (p. 23)) but by so often describing visual features as forms of writing or vision itself as a form of reading: 'I really can name nothing out of the way' remarks Mr Enfield of Hyde. 'No, sir; I can make no hand of it; I can't describe him' (p. 15); Utterson refers to 'Satan's signature upon a face' (p. 23) (that of Hyde) and the narrator comments upon a 'death-warrant written legibly upon [Dr Lanyon's] face' (p. 41); Jekyll, upon looking in the mirror, sees 'evil ... written broadly and plainly on the face of [Hyde] ... an imprint of deformity and decay' (p. 73). This same mirror which reflects not revealed truth but written signs, that reveals seeing as but reading, is the one Utterson and Poole gaze into on Jekyll's last night and which, no doubt having witnessed the very transformation Jekyll himself is incapable of narrating, 'was so turned as to show them nothing', nothing, that is, 'but the rosy glow playing on the roof, the fire sparkling in a hundred repetitions along the glazed front of the presses' – repetition not revelation – and an image figuring Utterson's unease 'and their own pale and fearful countenances stooping to look in' (p. 58). The looking *in* becomes a looking *at*, readers confronting a problem of reading, a suggestion more fully confirmed by the exchange which follows: ' "This glass has seen some strange things, sir," whispered Poole. "And surely none stranger than itself" echoed the lawyer in the same tone' (p. 58).

The mirroring of Poole and Utterson's manner of address is in an exchange upon self-reflection where there is nothing to reflect but repetition.

There has been an equally long-standing opposition between speech and writing, and speech, like vision, can itself be seen as a form of writing. Poole triumphantly declares on Jekyll's last night that he has been 'twenty years in this man's house' and cannot be 'deceived about his voice' (p. 50), but Jekyll/Hyde is a forger (playing on an opposite meaning, as in 'bind') of more than cheques, wills and missives and is capable of acts of ventriloquism. There is a moment in the story, however, when speech attempts to break free from the constraints of writing. The narrator comments upon one of Jekyll's letters that 'with a sudden splutter of the pen, the writer's emotion had broken loose' (p. 51), but the rhymed transformation of 'utter' (one recalls also the being said to 'mutter' in its 'struggle to be born' (p. 86)) issues necessarily in further script in which the writer appeals for what is irrecoverable, the 'unknown impurity' (p. 87): 'For God's sake . . . find me some of the old' (p. 51).

'NAME YOUR FIGURE' (pp. 12–13)

If Stevenson's story is indeed 'about' narration, it is a subject, difficult as it is, which students would do well to confront, but in more accessible fashion, as I have tried to show here, than through overtly theoretical discussion of signifiers and signifieds, *fabula* and *sjuzhet*. The subject of narration necessarily affirms the textuality of story through a story of textuality, the partial narrativizing of experience hidden from the eye/I. As indicated and illustrated above, the textuality of fictional space in Stevenson's story can also be addressed through a study of tropes and figures, the play of reference as it transforms not merely faces into sheets of paper, eyes into lights and beacons, but in an apposite Stevensonian 'reversal' (p. 78), transfigures a lamp into a 'carbuncle' (p. 37), a wall into a 'blind forehead' (p. 11), as the soul, Utterson reflects, might be said to 'transpire through, and transfigure, its clay continent' (p. 23), as it suggestively places Jekyll at a window 'the middle one of the three . . . half way open' (p. 45) at a point midway through his journey of experimentation. Stevenson's story operates through the figuration of the literal and the literalizing of the meta-phorical, as Jekyll is himself, obscurely, the 'unknown impurity' (p. 87), some of the 'old' (p. 51). As words are themselves a product of translation, an utterance of thought or sensation, so once deployed, they effect transformations of reference, erupting like Hyde, sometimes 'doubl[ing] up' (p. 53), as when Jekyll reflects that some chemical agents have the power to 'pluck back that fleshly vestment, even as a wind might toss the curtains of a pavilion' (p. 71).

Every detail of geographical space, physiognomical attribute, meteorological condition, of streets and buildings, rooms and furnishings, faces and voices, of fog, wind, cloud and sunshine, has its relation to the psychological study in the story. Students view with enjoyment and more or less unhealthy cynicism (the questionable charge of 'reading in' can be routinely invoked) the play of reference to be had with words such as 'opposite' (p. 26), 'pair' (p. 14), 'broken' (pp. 23, 48, 55, 57), 'composure' (pp. 19, 66), 'Gaunt' (pp. 22, 34) and 'disinterred' (pp. 33, 55), with phrases such as 'a mixture of timidity and boldness' (p. 23), 'devilish little of the man' (p. 19), 'like a stain of breath upon a mirror' (p. 75) and 'a singular resemblance' (p. 38), and with remarks such as 'Utterson beheld a marvellous number of degrees and hues of twilight' (p. 31), Jekyll in a 'house of voluntary bondage ... confined himself to the cabinet' (p. 44), Enfield thought it 'impossible to do the one thing without the other' (p. 45). Other selves, other worlds and words haunt the legible surface, as Utterson is said to 'haunt the door in the by street of shops' (p. 20) in his guise as Mr Seek and as Hyde is figured by Utterson as 'the ghost of some old sin' (p. 25).

As Hyde proposes when attempting to pay off the outraged bystanders in the story's opening incident 'Name your figure' (pp. 12–13), it is, in another sense, the 'figure' of Hyde which is said to have 'haunted [Utterson] all night' as the 'scroll of lighted pictures' (p. 20), projections of his unconscious fears and fantasies (and indeed those of his 'friend' Jekyll), are played before him, a 'figure to whom power was given' (p. 20). In what ways, one must ask students to consider, is Utterson's 'imagination ... engaged, or rather enslaved' (p. 19) by the figure of Hyde? Here, in one of the story's many narrative enclosures, Utterson half-dreams of Jekyll dreaming until 'recalled' (p. 20), as he is himself; Utterson is 'enslaved' (p. 19) as Jekyll is said to be 'in bondage' to a figure which 'at that dead hour' exhorts him to 'rise' (p. 20), as Jekyll is later compared to 'a man restored from death' (p. 68) in his transformation from the figure of Hyde.

How might one read these reversals and replications which suggest a hidden master plot, a narrative of identification, projection and displacement?

'THE WAR IN THE MEMBERS'

To term Stevenson's story a 'psychological study' is the very least one can do. To develop the term so as to interrogate gender, family, sibling and Oedipal conflict is to push ahead with details the text does little to 'blazon' (p. 69) and as much to hide. In one of the most accomplished and substantial studies of the tale to date, 'Children of the Night: Stevenson and Patriarchy' (in *Dr Jekyll and Mr Hyde after 100 Years*, ed. Veeder and Hirsch, University of Chicago Press, 1988), William Veeder argues all too plausibly for the story as a study of the regressive emotions of Oedipal sons and sibling rivals. Veeder argues that Stevenson shows distinctions which ought to be maintained are elided, so that bonds occur where divisions should obtain; and affiliations that should be sustained are sundered, so that males war with one another and refuse to wed. In this account, Hyde is indeed the 'indifferent' son and Jekyll the 'interest(ed)' father engaged in a classic Oedipal struggle in which Hyde destroys the portrait of Jekyll's own father, Lanyon and Carew are themselves figured as 'fathers' and Utterson is the Utter-son who displaces Hyde as Jekyll's beneficiary. The punishment, death and injury of women and children are instances both of Oedipal anger and sibling rivalry, a rivalry no less noted as between Utterson and Hyde for command of Jekyll and his 'will'. Utterson, in Veeder's reading, is both the 'utter son', the devoted heir of patriarchy, and also the 'udder son' regressively oriented to the breast. The chemist 'Maw' is figured in this reading as the absent mother, 'some of the old' (p. 50), appropriated, as is so much else, by the male in 'Messrs Maw' (p. 51).

This argument, briefly rehearsed – or even if elaborated at length – will no doubt seem extravagant. But the wealth of biblical allusions, many of them from Genesis (to Cain and Abel, Isaac and Esau), are more suggestive of male familial conflicts than simply of the 'bands that God decreed to bind' in the famous epigraph to the story, which might encourage narrow Christian readings of the war between good and evil. Once students have appreciated that, as I have shown, the Jekyll/Hyde relationship is replicated throughout Jekyll's 'circle', but also, for example, that Poole has watery depths, that En(d)field is a man capable of stretching to the limits, that Den-man once occupied Jekyll's laboratory, it is not unreasonable to invite them to interrogate the terms of this relation in a way which suspends the familiar fixed terms of a binary opposition and the normative valuations of liberal/Christian frames of reference. It is precisely these terms, firmly fixed in place, which, in my experience, students all too readily bring to their readings of texts; Stevenson's story invites them – and as a teacher one should remain open to a reasoned account of how he might be said to confirm them – but, in my view, challenges them in the ways I have outlined above. Discussion and essay writing on the question of how far Stevenson is endorsing or questioning the 'bands' or 'bonds' that 'bind', is marking them as normative constraints or dangerous strictures, would be central in any programme of study.

'GO THEN, AND FIRST READ THE NARRATIVE' (p. 59)

It is in challenging and interrogating certain frames of reference that study of Stevenson's story is so rewarding. Opportunities abound for readings inflected by a concern with gender, class, even race (there are 'many women of many different nationalities passing out' (p. 32) in Soho); all such readings, along with those which foreground familial struggle or the uneasy relation between atavism and civilization, professionalism and domesticity are possible ways of figuring the conflicts within a classic Gothic text which situates the action in *fin-de-siècle* London. Such far from mutually exclusive approaches compel consideration because the story requires us to seek for the hidden, is indeed a search for meaning. The story is about reading, about how we construct character, plot and the codes of comprehension within narratives of experience or the experience of narrative. And it should be apparent from the density of a text which in its materiality and metaphoricity allows us to see double, as it were, that close textual work is imperative. Furthermore, the story's hybrid, labyrinthine narrative structure, its dispersal and encoding of stories and their sources of transmission, draw attention not merely to the constructedness of character and narrative, but ultimately to the partiality and provisionality of representation through narrative.

Beginning A-level study of narrative with Stevenson's story as an exemplar text (Conrad's *Heart of Darkness* is, as I have suggested, another) and, through it, introducing students to alternative ways of reading and understanding, even to theoretical perspectives of the kind I have outlined above, prepares them, of course, for reading across the genres (although poetry and drama might well be handled discretely in addition). But it encourages greater critical awareness of narrative strategy in particular. Students will be better equipped to deal with the narrative complexities of Emily Brontë's *Wuthering Heights*, the topographical densities of Charlotte Brontë's *Villette* or *Jane Eyre*, the incidence of the 'double' in Dickens's *Our Mutual Friend* or Conrad's *The Secret Sharer*. It will enable them to approach with more confidence and with greater critical acumen the vagaries of 'character' in Virginia Woolf or Angela Carter, the race and gender issues in Hardy and in Hawthorne, in Morrison and in Melville. It will further enable them to appreciate that texts are sites of enquiry rather than objects of study, modes of response rather than models of good practice; that reading – close reading – is not closed upon meaning but open to a variety of inflections and ambivalences. Dr Jekyll's 'nameless situation' (p. 59) is one with which it has been found productive to start.

Chapter 8

Tennyson: Teaching a Dead Poet at A-Level

Martin Blocksidge

I have always found it easier to teach poetry at A-Level than either drama or the novel. I find it much more answerable to the needs of my pupils, and to many of the activities immediately suited to the classroom. A poem, especially in comparison with a nineteenth-century novel, for example, is a finite thing. There is no doubt as to what we are looking at, and we are, in physical terms at least, all looking at the same thing. A teaching group of between ten and fifteen pupils is a natural seminar. Seminar conditions can be the norm from day one of the A-Level course and, in studying poetry, pupils can quickly grow used to the practice of questioning the poem, questioning each other and questioning me. Hence I normally choose to start my A-Level course with the study of a poet, preferably an unfamiliar one, preferably a 'dead' one.

One of the things which such an approach does is to signify a change of direction from GCSE. Until recently, it was unlikely that the GCSE experience of English literature would involve the sustained study of one particular poet's work, especially if that poet had lived and written before 1900. Recent changes have modified this situation, but only to a degree. While it is now certain that candidates will have met a greater diversity of poems than once used to be the case, it is likely that they will have done so by means of an anthology, possibly of the work of several poets, or possibly thematically organized. Once upon a time it was not very likely that pupils would have met 'The Lady of Shalott' or 'Morte d'Arthur'. These days they might well have done, if only as an act of tokenism in meeting the details of the National Curriculum requirements. The opportunity is still open for a broader and deeper approach to a poet such as Tennyson.

We are told that both teachers and students are frightened of poetry: it is seen as complex, remote and hermeneutically more teasing than fiction or drama, both of which are, in a variety of forms, freely available to everyone. I have more than once heard university teachers of English assert (or bemoan) the fact that their students do not have any real acquaintance with poetry written before 1900. I like to teach Tennyson not only to banish this slur from my own pupils, but because I think that studying him reflectively and in detail opens up many important aspects of critical practice.

Tennyson is less widely studied at A-Level than he might be. I suspect that this is not because he is viewed as 'difficult'; the surface of his work is not forbidding, as, for example, that of Milton, Hopkins or Eliot might be. Tennyson was in his time, after all, very much a 'people's poet', which is where the problem lies. He is still very much associated with the Victorian era, the laureate of a rigid and unsmiling society of whose values (*pace* Mrs Thatcher) the twentieth century has been suspicious. Critics of the first half of the century were notably hard on Tennyson. Leavis, in *New Bearings in English Poetry* (1932), banished him completely from serious consideration; Auden in 1944 accepted that he had 'the finest ear, perhaps, of any English poet', but then dismissed him as 'undoubtedly the stupidest'. Harold Nicolson in 1923 went in a different direction:

> the application of the Freudian system to the case of Tennyson is quite illuminating. For Tennyson was afraid of a great many things: predominantly he was afraid of sex and death and God. And in all these matters he endeavoured instinctively to sublimate his terrors by enunciating the beliefs which he desired to feel, by dwelling upon the solutions by which he would like to be convinced.

A little Freud can be a dangerous thing, and Nicolson belonged to the generation which enjoyed constructing an image of the Victorians against which it could then enjoy rebelling. Nicolson does move the argument on, however. While one might not be comfortable for long with the idea of Tennyson being a 'case', Nicolson does at least suggest that there is more to him than a fine ear and a pleasant surface. He opens up the possibility of reading Tennyson in a way which identifies the more interesting things in the poetry as happening subterraneously. The poetry is seen as compact of more dynamic elements which can benefit from closer analysis.

But the literary critic needs to separate analysis from psychoanalysis. Tennyson's fears and doubts; his uncertainties before the questions which the nineteenth century was believed to be certain about; the difficulty of accommodating his own feelings: these features have all helped in the rehabilitation of Tennyson within twentieth-century taste, particularly as there is no longer any imperative to view such concerns as pathological. Tennyson's scepticism about the very processes of creation has a strikingly modern feel to it:

> I sometimes hold it half a sin
> To put in words the grief I feel
> For words, like Nature, half reveal
> And half conceal the Soul within.

This stanza ('In Memoriam', V) is a good starting point for an appreciation of how Tennyson viewed his writing, but it is not the place I would choose to start in presenting his work to A-Level students. Rather than begin with a poem which talks of the relationship between words and 'meaning', I would begin with one which treats of depth and surface. I have already suggested that, in the critical sense, Tennyson offers an opportunity to consider the relationship between these two things. Just as he invites, in the 'In Memoriam' stanza quoted above, his readers to ponder on the process by which that poem was created, so in 'The Kraken' he offers an image of how his poetry may be read:

> Below the thunders of the upper deep;
> Far, far beneath in the abysmal sea,
> His ancient, dreamless, uninvaded sleep
> The Kraken sleepeth; faintest sunlights flee
> About his shadowy sides: above him swell
> Huge sponges of millennial growth and height;
> And far away into the sickly light,
> From many a wondrous grot and secret cell
> Unnumbered and enormous polypi
> Winnow with giant arms the slumbering green.
> There hath he lain for ages and will lie
> Battening upon huge seaworms in his sleep,
> Until the latter fire shall heat the deep;
> Then once by man and angels to be seen,
> In roaring he shall rise and on the surface die.

> > (Ricks, p. 246. All quotations are from *Poems of Tennyson*, ed. Ricks, Longman, 1969)

I have found that even quite young pupils are quick to appreciate that this poem can be read non-literally. A-Level students swiftly perceive that it is a poem which is open to interpretation. I have to say that I don't mind how my pupils choose to read it. When I started teaching Tennyson twenty-five years ago, we were all much closer to the pathological model of Tennyson (and of the Victorians generally) than we are now, and we were likely to see the poem as being about guilt: about the suppression of something (to the author, at least) dreadful. Most certainly the beast at the bottom of the sea is more powerful by far than anything else around it; even than the element in which it is contained. Those with a little Freud might talk of the relationship between the conscious and the subconscious mind; those with a bit more Freud might even get so far as 'the return of the repressed'. However, two features of the poem I wish to draw attention to are, first, that it is a poem of hypothesis and speculation: the Kraken does *not* rise to the surface, it is merely believed that he will. (Does this open up a Christian reading?) Second, the poem, although it ends in a climax, is in other respects inconclusive. It offers no comment on the *significance* of the Kraken's rising nor on the *consequence* of it. The conclusion is abrupt and unresolved, describing as it does something which has not yet happened.

The poems which I read with my students first tend to be the ones which Tennyson wrote first. This is not because I opt for an explicitly chronological view of his work, but because it is possible to find correspondences and patterns in the early poems which are well worth pursuing, the more so as they are not always obvious. Indeed, on the level of form and tone students are far more likely to be struck first by the differences than the similarities.

'The Kraken' and 'Mariana' were both published in 1830, when Tennyson was 21, though neither poem sounds particularly like apprentice work. 'Mariana' is too long to quote in its entirety. A brief synopsis will suffice. The poem is prefaced by a stark little reference to *Measure for Measure*: 'Mariana in the moated grange.' That is all. What follows is an evocation of Mariana's physical location and also of her mental state. Structurally for much of the time, the poem sounds almost like a list:

> The doors upon their hinges creaked;
> The blue fly sung in the pane; the mouse
> Behind the mouldering wainscot shrieked ...

What readers quickly begin to perceive is the way in which Mariana's physical surroundings and her mental state fuse. The things which are accessible to the senses, the sights and sounds of the house, are also those things which define Mariana's feelings and fears:

The sparrow's chirrup on the roof,
The slow clock ticking, and the sound
Which to the wooing wind aloof
The poplar made, did all confound
Her sense.

The nearest we get in the poem to any explanation of how Mariana comes to be where she is is in the refrain at the end of each verse: ' "He cometh not," she said.' We do not know who 'he' is, nor the reasons for his absence, though his desertion of Mariana is corrosive: the nails in the wall are 'rusted'; the poplar tree has 'gnarled bark' and the waters in the moat are 'blackened'. The physical atmosphere is rotting, and so, by extension, is Mariana herself. As we have seen, the ticking of the clock and the chirrup of the sparrow, rather than being reassuring, combine to 'confound her sense', and we can see this process developing when the mouse 'shrieked'. Mice do not shriek: Mariana's balance and control have been attacked by her imprisonment.

The poem offers no escape. Mariana is left, as she was found, enclosed and deprived of any company save normally inanimate objects and the sounds of animals. As with 'The Kraken', it does not take A-Level students long to realize that the poem needs to be 'read' in some way. As a 'realistic' piece of scene-setting it will not quite do, and students will want to examine it further.

Once more, a number of different interpretations present themselves: the poem can be seen as a description of someone going mad, losing their grip on the basic rhythms of life such as the passing of day and night. Another reading might well stress the sexual suggestiveness of the poem. We know that, above all, Mariana is deprived of a 'he' (any 'he' or a particular one?). Mariana's room has a virginally 'white curtain' at its window, and the repetitions of the verbs 'to come' and 'to die' at the end of each stanza remind us that both verbs bring sexual connotations with them. One critic (Marian Shaw, *Alfred Lord Tennyson* (Harvester Wheatsheaf, 1988)) suggests that Mariana can be seen to represent nineteenth-century womanhood in general:

> Mariana is herself the type of the lovelorn, waiting woman, but she is also more than that ... Mariana invokes all the other types of woman with which Victorian ideology will be concerned, an ominous and seductive questioner of the fate of womankind ... and her dependence on a man for release emphasises: 'the instatement of masculinity and the upholding of male power'.
>
> (p. 109)

The foregrounding of these issues points us next in the direction of 'The

Lady of Shalott'. Indeed, I often suggest this poem as a solution/sequel/ corollary to 'Mariana'. The Lady herself has one alternative which is not available to Mariana: escape. Although it is the Lady who exists explicitly under the threat of a curse, Mariana is the character who seems cursed, for whatever reason, to remain fixed where she is. 'The Lady of Shalott' offers escape as punishment to the Lady. The sexual saviour denied to Mariana appears, and as Sir Lancelot does so, the very language of the poem changes, moving from clear-edged pictorialism to something far more highly charged:

> The helmet and the helmet-feather
> Burned like one burning flame together . . .

> As often through the purple night,
> Below the starry clusters bright,
> Some bearded meteor, trailing light,
> Moves over still Shalott.   (p. 358)

Likewise, the Lady's submission to this almost visionary presence and her acknowledgement that the curse is upon her transform the physical environment of the poem. The curse disrupts the disciplined and ordered passage of images through the Lady's mirror. The natural world, like the Lady herself, seems to have become emancipated and ungovernable:

> In the stormy east-wind straining,
> The pale yellow woods were waning,
> the broad stream in his banks complaining.
> Heavily the low sky raining
> Over towered Camelot;
> Down she came and found a boat
> Beneath a willow left afloat,
> And round about the prow she wrote
> *The Lady of Shalott*.   (p. 359)

The Lady asserts her individuality at the moment of her destruction, and her destruction is, it seems to me, undeniably the result of her submission to the calls of human companionship represented through the sexual impulse. It had been the reflection of the 'two young lovers lately wed' which had caused the Lady to register her first words of rebellion.

Once again 'The Lady of Shalott' invites students to develop their own readings. It is possible, for example, to think more precisely about what the Lady herself represents. Isolated in her tower (itself a suggestive location), she 'weaves by night and day/a magic web'. Her work sounds both impressive and unremitting. It is almost as if she has been cursed to labour at the creation of a beautiful but never to be completed object. She can be seen as an artist, pursuing her own lonely vision, and nourished in it by that very withdrawal from human society against which she ultimately rebels.

Both 'Mariana' and 'The Lady of Shalott' consider the question of action. Mariana withers through her inability to act, and the Lady is destroyed as the result of taking action. The question of whether to act or to submit is presented more explicitly, though ultimately inconclusively, in 'The Lotos-Eaters'. It is also the subject matter, though approached from a very different angle, of 'Locksley Hall'. I would normally expect to give some time to both these poems at this point, before pausing for thought about one or two more general questions.

The first of these questions could well be the intentionalist one. How much of all this, especially where we have identified alternative readings or open-endedness, did Tennyson *intend*? This is a question which students can pose at any time, and with varying degrees of intelligence or even hostility. It is a question which all serious students of literature need to face at some time: if we accept that texts may have multiple meanings or that they are susceptible to different kinds of interpretation, we need to be clear about why we think this. It would be inappropriate to rehearse the arguments on the intentionalist question here, but it is true, I think, that the study of these early Tennyson poems enables students to see the limits of a crude intentionalism very easily, especially as the poems in question seem to invite the very kind of interpretive ingenuity which intentionalism distrusts. I would also point out that Tennyson himself was an intentionalist, extremely distrustful of alternative readings of his poems. This issue becomes crucial in any discussion of 'Ulysses', the poem I would discuss next with students.

Two other matters tend, without much forcing, to arise at this point too. The first is the extent to which it is possible to read the poems as biographical. I am in general loath to lard my teaching of poetry with too many biographical facts. Some are unavoidable (Pope's deformity, Hopkins's membership of the Society of Jesus), but they can all too easily be held *against* the poets by those who know nothing other than the isolated facts. That Tennyson had a notoriously difficult and unhappy childhood and young adulthood is well known, though to what extent the poems which we have read can be seen to reflect a pathological state of mind is questionable. I think it is important not to submit Tennyson to the kind of patronizing quasi-Freudianism of Harold Nicolson: the facts of his life might seem to encourage this, but any general tendency to view Tennyson's poems as merely morbid and neurotic is limiting.

A way in which I would wish to develop the biographical question is to move beyond it. A point I should almost certainly wish to make about early Tennyson is that his writing is very *literary*. Literariness in an author is often seen as adding an extra skin of complexity to what is being done. The allusiveness of T.S. Eliot, for example, can be seen by a novice reader as discouraging, even gratuitous. In Tennyson this is not so. Indeed, the extent of his literariness is often not recognized by students until it is pointed out to them, when, of course, certain patterns begin to emerge. All the poems discussed above have relationships with already existing narratives. Spending a little time on considering these relationships is valuable, especially in the context of the other general issues I have raised.

Tennyson's habit is to take an existing story and appropriate its characters and incidents to the point where they break free of their origins. Mariana in Shakespeare's *Measure for Measure* is lodged in the moated grange, having been jilted by Angelo. We meet her in the play only when she is invited to leave the grange and return to Angelo. There is no suggestion that she has suffered; there is no suggestion at all about the nature of the moated grange, and the fact that Tennyson's poem seems to admit no possibility of escape for Mariana is completely at odds with Shakespeare. Comparably, the Lotos-Eaters in Tennyson convince themselves that it would be best to remain on the enchanted island rather than return home with Ulysses, whereas in *The Odyssey* Ulysses compels them to return. Tennyson explained that the story of *The Lady of Shalott* originated in 'an Italian novella'. However, the original story is significantly different: 'it has no Arthur, Queen, mirror, weaving, curse, song, river or island' (Ricks, p. 354). All the most important features of Tennyson's story are his own. Tennyson's characters seem suspended in time and space, experiencing emotions which lie just beyond what is explicable by an easy appeal to experience or reason. In these poems Tennyson himself is invisible. The poems have been created in a literary context which might seem to explain them and then wrenched away from it.

I have already expressed some doubts about the policy of pursuing a too explicitly biographical reading of Tennyson, but there is one biographical fact which needs to be faced: the death of his friend, Arthur Hallam, in 1833. The intensity, and indeed diversity, of Tennyson's reactions to this event can sometimes be difficult for students to grasp. They either think that Tennyson was simply over-reacting, or they assume that he and Hallam must have been gay. Biographers have found no conclusive evidence on the latter point and I find it best not to spend too much time pursuing it, in order to prevent Tennyson from becoming either a hostage to homophobic prejudice or condemned for staying in the closet.

Of the poem 'Ulysses', Tennyson wrote: 'There is more about myself in *Ulysses*, which was written under the sense of loss and that all had gone by, but that still life must be fought out to the end.' If a discussion of Tennyson's poems has not thus far embraced intentionalism, this is the moment at which it will unavoidably do so. It is clearly possible to read 'Ulysses' in a way consistent with the comments which Tennyson made about it. The last lines, often quoted out of context, are suggestive in their masculine exhortation to action:

> that which we are, we are;
> One equal temper of heroic hearts,
> Made weak by time and fate, but strong in will
> To strive, to seek, to find, and not to yield.   (p. 566)

I would wish, quite explicitly, to ask my students to read this poem against the grain. Indeed, I can think of few poems which more urgently require to be read in this way. The more sophisticated readers, particularly those growing attuned to verbal detail, will almost certainly need little encouragement. They will note again the literary origin of the poem, though they will need to have the fact pointed out that the Ulysses of this poem is Dante's elderly hero and not Homer's more youthful one. It is interesting that Tennyson, aged 24, is explicitly identifying in this poem with an elderly man, a man whose tone of voice at the beginning of the poem is represented as grumbling and ungenerous:

> It little profits that an idle king,
> By this still hearth, among these barren crags,
> Matched with an aged wife, I mete and dole
> Unequal laws unto a savage race,
> That hoard, and sleep, and feed, and know not me.   (p. 561)

Ulysses's view of his kingdom, his subjects, even his wife, is unflattering, almost contemptuous. A similar tone of voice returns when, later in the poem, Ulysses describes his son Telemachus, implying that he is a small enough man to find satisfying the daily duties of government which so irk him. Ulysses's desire for travel is in part at least motivated by a boredom with his daily existence:

> How dull it is to pause, to make an end,
> To rust unburnished, not to shine in use.   (p. 563)

That Ulysses is excited by the prospect of travel is clear enough, but the poem is crucially vague about where he sees his journey actually taking him. He seems to find difficulty in disentangling the memory of past voyages from the anticipation of future ones:

> Yet all experience is an arch wherethrough
> Gleams that untravelled world, whose margin fades
> For ever and for ever when I move.   (p. 563)

The untravelled world is vague and shifting. Ulysses images his voyage asymptotically. He conceives of its course but not of its destination:

> To follow knowledge like a sinking star,
> Beyond the utmost bound of human thought.   (p. 563)

The nature of Ulysses's final journey is as mind-boggling as it is ill-defined. It is also more glamorous in general than in specific terms. When Ulysses looks out at the sea which is facing him, the poem's mood grows more sombre: 'There *gloom* the dark broad seas ... The long day *wanes* ... the deep/*Moans* round with many voices' (pp. 564–5). The italics are mine, but the verbs concerned do not suggest an inviting prospect. By setting the final part of the poem in the moonlight, Tennyson reverses the conventional imagery of departure. A feeling of closure rather than opening is developed, and is indeed almost stated:

> Death closes all: but something ere the end,
> Some work of noble note, may yet be done.   (pp. 564–5)

Something *may* be done, but Ulysses is extremely vague about what. Both his imagery and tone of voice colour the final lines of the poem. They are introduced by a series of emphatic concessive clauses: 'Though much is taken, much abides and though' (p. 565).

The final assertion is hedged about by uncertainties. The poem betrays its narrator's lack of resolve and purpose. The voice has a strange mixture of romantic longing and irritability, features which subvert each other. The poem thus becomes a study not of 'braving the struggle of life' but of the difficulty of making that struggle at all: it is a struggle to which not even Ulysses, symbolic superman, is finally equal. It is a poem which both contemplates and represses the idea of failure. It presents exhilarating prospects hemmed in by present weaknesses and disabilities.

'Morte d'Arthur' is the other poem in which Tennyson registers, through an appropriated fictional narrative, a complex reaction to Hallam's death. Tennyson, as laureate, became celebrated for his Arthurian writing in 'Idylls of the King', to which a slightly modified version of 'Morte d'Arthur' was to form the conclusion (I have offered a more detailed reading of 'Morte d'Arthur' in an article in *The English Review*, Vol. 2, No. 4, April 1992). As with 'Ulysses', Tennyson's attitude to his literary material in this poem is not simply reverential. Just as Ulysses is not granted an unequivocally heroic status, so King Arthur and Sir Bedevere both behave in ways which are open to censure.

As pure narrative, 'Morte d'Arthur' is one of Tennyson's best-known poems. Indeed, the vigour and precision of its story-telling make it accessible to pupils of almost any age. What I would seek to do here is to register some of the features of it which seem particularly characteristic of Tennyson's writing in the context of the poems discussed above. As we might expect, Tennyson has some significant changes to make to the story which comes originally from Sir Thomas Malory. To start with, Tennyson desolates the scene. The battle from which Arthur and Bedevere emerge as sole survivors seems very much to be the final battle, a holocaust:

> The bold Sir Bedevere uplifted him . . .
> And bore him to a chapel nigh the field,
> A broken chancel with a broken cross,
> That stood on a dark strait of barren land.
> On one side lay the Ocean and on one
> Lay a great water.   (p. 586)

Just as Tennyson enclosed Mariana in a physical world which seemed to offer no hope of escape, so he places Arthur and Bedevere in a setting which seems to offer no possibility of reconstruction or renewal. This feeling is apprehended particularly by Bedevere who, in Tennyson's version of the story, becomes the central figure. The poem is complicit with Bedevere's inability to obey Arthur and dispose of the sword Excalibur, the final symbol of Arthur's kingship. Although the poem deals with the last moments in Arthur's life, and foregrounds Bedevere as the only loyal knight who is left, the two men seem at odds with each other rather than reconciled to a common fate. Not only does Bedevere disobey his king's commands twice, but he is only forced into loyalty by Arthur's threat of physical violence upon him. Likewise at his moment of departure to the 'island-valley of Avilion', Arthur seems unable to offer Bedevere any comfort at all. The revelation about the future which Bedevere so much needs is denied him:

> The old order changeth, yielding place to new,
> And God fulfils himself in many ways,
> Lest one good custom should corrupt the world.
> Comfort thyself: what comfort is in me?   (pp. 595–6)

The poem is, in its ending, not a comfortable one. Its highly atmospheric narrative cannot conceal the fact that its subject is the disconsolate mourner from whom Arthur must depart and to whom he will never return. Once again, Tennyson has intervened in an existing story (in this case a well-known one) and adapted it to mirror his own concerns.

In this study I have not dealt with Tennyson the eminent Victorian. Indeed, all the poems which I have discussed were written before Victoria became Queen. Like Wordsworth, Tennyson has often been thought to have 'gone off' in his later years. This is unfair, though it is significantly more difficult to find a body of poems from Tennyson's later career which form such a coherent group as those published before 1842. Also like Wordsworth, Tennyson, as he grew older, tended to interest himself in lengthier projects. At different times, I have taught both 'In Memoriam' and 'Maud' in their entirety. Both can be seen as daunting undertakings. 'In Memoriam' (as, I suspect, my students very quickly appreciated) is not easy to encompass, particularly as the issues which are registered in 'Ulysses' and 'Morte d'Arthur' become diffused in 'In Memoriam', and the poem's never quite fulfilled quest for a climax can be worrying. I think that 'In Memoriam' contains a great deal of Tennyson's most illuminating writing, but it is not an obvious text for A-Level use. At least some of the collections of Tennyson's verse which are available for students contain extracts from the poem, and it can be useful to sample these as an attempt to understand something of its flavour.

'Maud' is a different matter. Limitations of space prevent a detailed discussion of it here, but I have found that students respond readily to its power and directness, particularly after they have had time to work on some of Tennyson's more obviously approachable poems. The narrating voice of the 'monodrama' is an interesting subject in itself, as is the presentation of 'Maud' as a series of distantly glimpsed fragments.

Tennyson has much to offer A-Level students. As I suggested at the outset of this chapter, I have found him a particularly useful poet to read at the beginning of an A-Level course (preferably as a 'coursework text' rather than for examination). Not only does he give students an opportunity for some genuinely investigative critical reading, he opens up new experiences of the way in which poetry can work. A student begins to learn, through the study of him, a greater variety of reading strategies. He/she can begin to appreciate that the poet is often, in the end, invisible and that reading poetry is not simply a question of successive variations on the theme of 'I feel . . .'. In addition, despite the biographical prompting of some of his work, the reader of Tennyson is encouraged to interrogate and interpret the text as an end in itself. As I have suggested, too, the student almost certainly needs to question some of his/her lingering assumptions about intentionalism, and to appreciate that it is a legitimate activity to read a text against its grain. In this chapter I have not suggested that any reading of the poems discussed is the only one available, but I hope that I have shown that by asking certain questions about them they repay close study.

Chapter 9

A Beam of Light and a Pair of Boots
Drama texts at A-Level

Martin Hayden

Imagine a small theatre: no more than a rectangular open space, really, a little larger than an average village hall. An upper-level gallery contains the only seats. Most of the audience are standing in the space staring up at the magical lights and the everyday artisan's objects suspended from the ceiling, or at the banners and flags of working people's clubs and unions displayed from the upper levels and around the sides. The audience gradually become aware that some of the people mixing with them *are* the actors, mostly dressed in working clothes, or a simple costume. A band in the gallery start up a lively folk tune, the actors clear a space and perform a dance. When they have finished this relaxed, exuberant physical warm-up, a sustained organ chord abruptly changes the mood, and a fork-lift truck enters from one corner, with, standing on the top, in a white cassock, God, who begins to declaim (but in a Yorkshire accent!): 'Ego sum alpha et omega ...'

My wife and two small sons were at this performance, in the Cottesloe Theatre, of *The Nativity* from the National Theatre's version of the *Mysteries*, just after Christmas in 1984. The 'promenade' approach meant that, at ground level, you followed the action round different parts of the space, saw some scenes from a distance, some not at all, some where you were almost on top of the actors. Occasionally we were told to sit down – on the hard floor! My wife was pregnant with our third child at the time and decided, with our youngest in tow, to opt for the seats upstairs. Our 10-year-old stayed with me and got as involved as he could: holding a pencil-torch 'candle' aloft with all the other children who encircled Mary at the moment of nativity, or throwing a wet sponge at Mak the Sheep-stealer in the stocks, or sitting so close to the actors in the Herod scene that Herod moved threateningly towards *him* as he gave his order for the slaughter of the innocents. The audience had an especially full and deep involvement: for example, at one point when we had been encouraged to sit down, Gabriel, played by a black actor in a resplendent white robe, appeared on the upper level holding a large circular mirror, with which he reflected an intense beam of light down on to the acting area, letting it brush over the audience a little, until he concentrated it on a woman sitting next to me, who cupped her hand over her eyes. I remember thinking, 'That's a bit much, *some* audience participation's all well and good, but it's not fair to inflict such dazzling light on a member of the audience for so long!' The woman stirred in a dazed manner and stood up, and then I realized why she had been singled out: she was the actress playing Mary.

The specialness of that occasion for me had to do with the coming together of many things: the old story, with its resonance of the sacred, and its place at the heart of our culture; the production, with its imaginative re-creation of a sense of the communal, and its celebration of ordinary people, while it was *at the same time* activating the mythic dimension through the wonderful variety of methods proper to theatre, as rendered through the vision of the director Bill Bryden and the art of the actors; our presence there with two small children, and our expected third child. It is perhaps salutary to realize that it is only at *this* stage that I think of a *text*, or remember that there was a text! Drama at best is about collaborative creation. It is good to start by remembering that: the *experience* in the theatre on that night in late December was immediate and unrepeatable. It represented what we should keep in mind when studying drama texts at A-Level: in the classroom, in the studio even, we are only working around the peripheries of that kind of essential experience. One finds *one* major source of the experience by turning to the text used, which in that case was of course Tony Harrison's reworking and rearranging of several medieval English texts; 'reworking' is I think the right term, because it was not a rendering into modern English, but an attempt to create a hybrid dramatic language with a northern dialect feel, and with the stylized stress patterns and alliteration of the originals, and retaining an unashamedly unmodern vocabulary. In fact I have to admit that the *text* disappoints me a little in that it reminds me of Dr Johnson's stricture on Milton, that 'he wrote no language'. Here we have a language little related to any English ever spoken anywhere, I suspect. So, if I'm right, here's a little cautionary tale: great theatre doesn't necessarily need great texts, and, as we English teachers know, as veterans of so many productions of *Macbeth* and *Romeo and Juliet*, the converse can also be true.

Nevertheless, Bill Bryden in a television interview around the time of

The Mysteries offered the opinion that in quality as drama, the original plays are second only to Shakespeare in English. This may be so: it may well be that the deepest, most profoundly absorbing drama is always in touch with the mythic dimension, never completely out of reach of ritual, and communal celebration.

I like to introduce the Mystery Plays to a class by saying that they tell the whole story, or are the story of everything, and then say, after a pause: from the creation to the end of the world. Not 'politically correct' of course (a fact underlined by the most recent production of *The Mysteries* by the RSC in Stratford, which transferred, in a changed and 'corrected' version, I gather, to London) but the way the stories open out worlds of the imagination and spirit at the same time as they concentrate the experience of the suffering, fallible human beings, the ease with which they allow comedy but switch without warning into anguish or grimness, is surely something to do with where the stories come from, how, through the work of centuries, they have been adapted and re-invented, and made endlessly resilient. We should continue that process. Ask the students how *they* would start the sequence, suggest the 'creation' through dramatic means. How *they* would present God talking to Noah. What music would they use for the building of the ark? Or for the nativity?

Another much more ancient text that works, in translation, with sixth-formers is Sophocles's *Oedipus the King*. Its story has a direct, concentrated power, inseparable from the extreme economy of the means by which it is conveyed. The degree of concentration seems to be in inverse proportion to the imaginative range. It develops in one place and at one time with an effect of spontaneous immediacy and its essence is simple: all through, the drama is in the intensifying irony that, repeatedly, the one who tries to help, or to forestall, makes things worse.

Sophocles's dramatic art is one of a subtle telescoping of scenes, developments and even characters. The story is always plunging us forward into the next stage. For example, Jocasta, finding that Oedipus has accused Creon of plotting with the prophet Tiresias to overthrow him, tries to set her husband's mind at rest by giving what she thinks are good reasons to discount prophecy: the oracle that said her son should kill his father was not fulfilled. But she lets slip that her former husband Laius was murdered by thieves at a place where three roads cross – sufficient to jog Oedipus's memory and make him begin to realize, in one of those tersely worded but lengthy speeches of recall that are at the heart of the drama, that *he* is the killer. Similarly the dramatic use of the chorus repays study. They send for the shepherd who was the only survivor and witness of the killing of Laius. The audience wait in anticipation for what he will confirm while listening to the next chorus, but at its end Sophocles again suddenly pitches us ahead, as the messenger arrives from Corinth to announce the death of Oedipus's 'father' Polybus. Before long *he* is precipitating full realization of the unspeakable by trying to help: Oedipus mentions his horror of his 'homeland' ever since he had heard an oracle telling him that he would kill his father and mate with his mother, and, with cheerful confidence, the messenger quietens his fears: relax, Polybus and Merope were never your parents! And so it goes on: as in Sophocles's dramatic economy, this messenger doubles as the one who received the baby Oedipus from the palace servant, on Mount Citharon, and the palace servant in question is the one already sent for.

The strange almost unbearable power of this play works every time, with sixth-formers for example, because of the intensity of the concentration it embodies and generates. Each time the action jumps forward, the play enacts moments of realization, as, behind what is happening onstage, the audience creates in imagination the larger inner drama. Is this hinterland behind the text and action the mark of the greatest drama? Here, the experience is thrilling and awesome, despite what is horrible in the story.

A useful exercise with this play is to glance at the very long speech of the messenger who comes to tell of the death of Jocasta and the self-blinding of Oedipus: ask the students how they would do this on stage with a modern audience. They start to worry about how to keep their attention over such a long speech. After much discussion of the feasibility of accompanying it with mimed actions or tableaux as a backdrop, or dividing it up among speakers, we *read* it together, involve ourselves in its narrative power, and most students recognize that all it needs is to be well projected, as a speech, with no distractions from the vivid pictures it creates.

The ancient technique of *stychomythia*, where, at moments of greatest dramatic tension, characters speak in alternate single lines or even half-lines, can be easily identified in Fagles's translation (Penguin Classics, 1984), and its effects explored, practically in reading and performance, or by getting the students to imitate the technique in their own writing. Students will also enjoy developing part of a *stasimon* as choral speech: they learn a line each, say, of the first strophe of the second *stasimon*: 'Who – who is the man the voice of god denounces?', then decide on how to position the speakers on-stage, what gestures will be used, what style of delivery, and so on, and work it up for performance and/or videoing.

Such work on these two features of the play helps to bring out the twin poles of the drama: intense dramatic interaction in the scenes, as against momentary respite and the imaginative opening out of the story in the *stasimon*. The mythological, religious and cultural references of the latter are an education in themselves.

Where is the space in an English or English literature A-Level, as against drama or theatre studies, for the study of Greek drama? Should there be such a space? Not according to the new draft guidelines for A-Level courses, which insist on 'works originally written in English'. (I did *Antigone* for English A-Level myself, in 1960-something, and have never forgotten it.) If English *literature* is above all meant to offer a *literary* education, inclusive of drama, essential dimensions of the concept of drama are missing if students don't encounter the Greeks.

The Mystery Plays, like the plays of Shakespeare or Sophocles, emerge from the centre of a living culture: they are in some sense expressive of that unity of language, religion, custom, community and history. That National Theatre production seemed to achieve the miracle illusion of re-creating it for a brief space. We shouldn't underestimate what theatre can do, when we think of its origins and connections.

Now, we have a fragmented culture with no centre. We have something called a 'National Theatre' in London, but in reality it's just a building. There's much talk of Shakespeare, much teaching of him, lots of performances and films, but is our grip on him weakening or strengthening? This is not a subject for this chapter. Do we have a dramatist today writing plays which aim to speak from some kind of centre? Let's consider David Hare, whose trilogy on British institutions was performed at the National Theatre. I have been teaching *Murmuring Judges*, which is a set text on the AEB English course. Hare's play is worked up from research, from documentary materials, some of which have also been published; while telling the story of Gerard, a young Irishman in London who unwisely drifts into crime but is not yet a criminal, but whose harsh prison sentence is clearly destroying his life, it makes telling points about the judiciary, about the police in contemporary Britain, about crime, and about what desperate places prisons are. It shows the dramatist's ordering intelligence impressively at work (a *clarifying* intelligence), interrelating and contrasting the three worlds of the play through dramatic means: by swift movement from one to another; by presenting scenes from two or three of them simultaneously on stage; by freezing a scene on one side of the stage while a different scene continues on the other side and alternating between them; by inserting a brief moment (e.g. a Gerard monologue) into a scene essentially set in one of the other worlds, most memorably when, as guests assemble for a sumptuous feast in one of the Inns of Court, we switch from a Toastmaster calling out names of VIPs to

Gerard in his prison cell on one side of the stage, looking up at the grey square of light of his cell window:

> Six o'clock is the worst. That's when it hits you. When you sense the evening outside. Listening to the traffic. You were served your supper at four thirty. And now you're being told it's the end of the day.

Hare shows something of the artist-dramatist's gift for identifying with multiple points of view, giving us without too much sense of caricature the tone, attitudes and mores of a profession. So we get the blunt humour, innuendoes and 'digs' at the police station; the public school ethos and old boys' chumminess and rivalry on the Bench and Bar; and, in the prison, almost the most memorable character in the play is the prison officer Beckett, who speaks to Gerard with a gruff direct realism, offering blunt advice that is curiously not unsympathetic but somehow deadening to him and to us, emerging out of the prison situation as we are powerfully made to feel he knows it so well. To the visiting lawyer he says bleakly, out of his experience and cynicism:

> *Beckett*: We get a lot of visitors . . .
>   *Irina*: I'm sure.
> *Beckett*: Coming to look over this place. We have a name for them.
>   *Irina*: Oh yes. What's that?
> *Beckett*: We call them Something-Must-Be-Dones. Oh look, we say, there's another bunch of Something-Must-Be-Dones. This place is their monument.
>   *Irina*: And is nothing done?
>   (*He looks at her a moment, a sudden quiet flash of real feeling.*)
> *Beckett*: Only by us, Miss Platt. It's left to us.

Yet there's something just a little external, 'documentary' even, about the play. The main weakness is that the young black lawyer, Irina, is too obviously Hare's mouthpiece, as in the unconvincing scene where she attacks her boss, Sir Peter Edgecombe QC, and indicts the complacency of a profession. And the dialogue, naturalistic as it has to be, often seems strained and forced. Nevertheless, we had great fun trying out the terrific last scene of Act I, where against the background of the Overture to *The Magic Flute*, three scenes are presented simultaneously, one in the prison, one in the police station, and one, with Irina and Sir Peter, in the Royal Opera House, Covent Garden, and stage action has to match developments in the music. I brought in a recording, and it was exciting to discover that if you got it right the music did fit the action! And the student playing Gerard brooding in his prison cell, on the edge of the stage next to the lively social/cultural occasion at the opera in the centre, really brought home the theatrical effectiveness of that moment. At that point *not* documentary but theatrical, in the best sense.

If we have to view our culture as centreless and fragmented, perhaps the best plays today are those which recognize this fact, at least implicitly. David Storey clearly writes out of one fragment, perhaps Charlotte Keatley another . . . and Samuel Beckett?

There are three plays by Storey that I think are very fine: *The Contractor*, *Home*, and *The Changing Room*. The first and third make particularly inventive use of the theatre. For example, *The Changing Room* is indeed set in the changing room at a rugby league match, Act I before the game, Act II during the interval, Act III after the game. In a sense the play is all speech, people talking as they go about routinely preparing, resting and receiving attention, recovering and relaxing. Storey has the genuine novelist's/dramatist's gift to render speech, and natural instinctive or intuitive interest in human beings first and foremost: there are no interfering *ideas* or *theories* or *things to say* in his best plays. He doesn't have Hare's documentary ambition, if I can call it that; he is not trying to 'explore' the northern English institution of Rugby League and 'say' something about it: his creative gift is absorbed in rendering these lives at this moment. There are class issues, even political issues, in the play, but they arise with and through and in the subject matter: the slightly tawdry but also curiously impressive sense of superiority and ownership of Sir Frederick Thornton, the club chairman, who always has the club secretary MacKendrick as his dog-like attendant; the sense of a sharing of privilege with responsibility with the captain, Owen; the leadership and unquestioningly accepted authority of the coach and assistant coach, who relate in a freer, warmer way to the players than do Thornton and MacKendrick; the bringing together into male comradeship and intuitive 'togetherness' of people from diverse backgrounds and interests, held together, not without some tensions, through humour and a special kind of warmth/intimacy and familiarity. There is recognition of 'place' and authority, a finding of natural levels, and a quite delicate respect for differences and idiosyncrasies, which is clearly on the edge of feeling and attitudes that at other times would be bullying, or ostracizing, or cruel: the relationships are a delicate tension. Storey, attending to the 'living principle' here, his eye on the moment-by-moment rendering of the poetry of speech and relationship, creates a politics utterly remote from any *Guardian* liberal consensus, or any *Telegraph* ethos.

We can compare Hare's Sergeant, Lester Speed, in *Murmuring Judges*, also a large man in all respects, with Storey's Walsh. Walsh is loud and rather brashly simple and unshakeably himself. Humour is his element and male companionship his lifeblood, one suspects. (These days one has to make it clear that I make no reference to his sexuality here.) Lester has his crudities and there is a hint of minor racism at one point. But his enormous authority in the charge room, often dormant, explodes suddenly into anger that voices his fundamental decency and professionalism when he verbally attacks one Jason Smith, whose unsuccessful slightly drunken pleading to be let off a drink-driving charge had turned into abuse. The real drama that is at the heart of what Hare is about comes next, however. Suddenly contrite and apologetic, Jason kneels in front of Lester in the middle of the room, pleading again. There is a long, uncomfortable silence. Someone offers to make tea. Someone mutters, 'I hate it when they grovel.' The young policewoman, Sandra, entering, attempts humour: 'Hello, what's this? A proposal of marriage?' to which no one responds. Hare is interested in and has a sharp eye for how professional roles, functions and routines cut off the range of reactions and limit the full natural human response. The extreme uncomfortableness here is because no one *can* respond to Jason's human predicament ('I'm on my knees to you, skip. My wife and I, we're going through changes. Think. I'm a builder. I lose my licence, I tell you, I'm nothing ...'). Lester moves away without saying anything. This small moment mirrors nicely the larger issue of how the QC responds, or fails to respond, to Gerard as an individual case and as a human being, angering the young barrister Irina.

At the end of Storey's play, Walsh, having finally just left, is beautifully summed up in these remarks between the trainer and the club captain:

> *Crosby*: Not two bloody thoughts to rub together ... (*Gestures off.*)
> Walshy.
> *Owens*: No. (*Laughs.*)
> *Crosby*: Years ago ... ran into a bloody post ... out yonder ... split the
> head of any other man ... Gets up: looks round: says, 'By God',
> then ... 'Have they teken him off?'

What is interesting here is how what could be just a dismissive insult is, by the end of the passage, appreciative talk about Walsh: it is typical of the way the play achieves a warmth of shared humanity without a hint of sentimentality. I've used extracts from this play with English literature and theatre studies students on a number of occasions, and they are always intrigued by it, and it provokes exploratory discussion about their own experience of the dynamics of relationships and banter in teams and changing rooms.

The obvious contrast, or parallel, with Storey's evocations of male companionship and comradeship is Charlotte Keatley's *My Mother Said*

I Never Should. This is a fine play about four generations of women: great-grandmother Doris, grandmother Margaret, mother Jackie, and Rosie, the daughter. The interrelations are considerably complicated by the fact that Jackie's brief attempt to bring up her daughter on her own fails, and Rosie is brought up by Margaret, her grandmother, thinking she is her mother, while Jackie uneasily pursues a successful career as an artist. Doris, of the oldest generation, gave up her teaching job on marriage to be a housewife, though she is widowed in the course of the play. We see her daughter Margaret's excitement and idealism as she approaches marriage, but it is clear later that as a mother and housewife she is trying to fulfil herself through her daughter, urging her to give up the child to concentrate on her career, but also, in a complex of emotions, relishing the chance to mother her daughter's child. Later, Margaret tries to be a working mother and wife, but under strain, and the marriage breaks down. Eventually she dies of cancer just before Rosie's sixteenth birthday. The play is often very poignant, sometimes too freely emotional perhaps; at times it's grim and bleak, but ultimately it aims to be positive. Though no male character appears (at several points they are conveniently just off-stage), Doris in particular speaks powerfully and movingly of her relationship with 'Jack', especially of the time just before his death. Margaret is telling her mother about her separation from her husband:

> *Margaret*: Mummy, I still want him.
>   *Doris*: Your Father . . . stopped 'wanting me', many years ago. One didn't divorce, then. I thought if I persisted in loving him . . . I wanted to . . . to be desired. *(Pause.)* The night before he died, we embraced. He held my hand; he said that he loved me most that night. I believed him . . . Was it worth it, I ask myself? *(Silence.)* You've made more of your life. A job and that.

There is a directness and accessibility about this play, together with the way it constantly engages with what one might call life-issues, that make it immediately appealing to sixth-form students, and, as with Storey's best work, the play is inventive as a play. Various imaginative effects of parallel, contrast and link-up are achieved because in Act I the scenes are not chronological but jump about in time. Act II is largely one long scene, in which the four women are clearing the rather ghostly house in which Doris's husband Jack has recently died, and the objects, photos and clothes that turn up skilfully bring back the concerns of Act I for further development. The four characters also appear as themselves-as-children in a series of scenes evocative of women's experience somewhat spookily filtered through children's play. Ultimately, the play probably stands or falls on the character of Rosie, or even the success or failure of the vernacular that the author creates for her. The zest and vividness of her speech allows absolutely no sentimentality; she responds with an open, fresh honesty that is invigorating after the hesitancies, insecurities and occasional mendacity of the previous generations. It's hard to illustrate effectively in snatches, but the following gives a flavour of it:

> *Rosie*: . . . You're old enough to be my mum! I'm glad you're not.
> *Jackie*: Why?
> *Rosie*: Because it would be a mega-pain having to live up to you. Grandad used to go on and on about you, you know.
> *Jackie*: He disapproved of me.
> *Rosie*: He didn't.
> *Jackie*: I'm not how he thinks a woman should be.
> *Rosie*: That's what he liked! You are dumb.
> *Jackie (amazed)*: It wasn't admiration you know, his will! It was revenge.
> *Rosie*: How?
> *Jackie*: I'd escaped. Families. – Nearly. He's made me responsible for all of you now.
> *Rosie*: You are thick. He left you the money so you can open a gallery of your own.

Here Rosie is 11. Her freedom from the 'hang-ups' of the previous generations is well represented in her manner of reply and tone of voice. She chooses to live, after Margaret's death, not with her newly revealed 'real' mother Jackie, but with her great-grandmother, newly liberated into independence through widowhood. Rosie has a robustness that carries the author's hope for a better future for women. She solves the solitaire game in the final scene of the play, except that it is not *quite* the last scene: in a marvellous *coup*, the play ends with the *earliest* scene, in time, in which Doris, the oldest generation in the play but here speaking as a young woman, joyfully tells her mother of her engagement, and some other news:

> *And* Mother, *and* I got promoted to Head of Infants this morning! Miss Butterworth called me into her office, my heart was in my mouth, I thought she was going to tick me off for this dress being too short! . . . Jack was very proud when I told him, but of course he says I shan't need to work when we're – when we're – . . . Oh Mother, I'm so happy, SO HAPPY! I suppose, really and truly, this is the beginning of my life! (*Lights fade to a single spot on Doris, then snap out.*)

We hear the joy but feel simultaneously the pain of expectations unfulfilled, opportunities given up, the frailty, perhaps, of such joyful setting out: the extreme poignancy communicates itself immediately to any group, and they talk about the scene spontaneously. Each of the four characters has a monologue at some points, excellent material for theatre studies activities, or as stimulus for coursework creative tasks in English: the scope of the play can be indicated, a sample of scenes read (this is a play you will find the students want to take away and finish on their own, anyway), then the four monologues studied, and the students prepared to produce their own set, evoking the lives of a family group, or the experiences and attitudes of different generations. Though I don't wish to suggest that it's on the same level, the play has clear relationships with the television 'soap opera' genre, and there are links to explore here too: the scene where Margaret comes to collect the baby from Jackie can be read, and the students (it could be another English coursework task, or a starting point for media studies students) set to imagine a soap opera context for it.

Male comradeship or rivalry in the north of England, the life experiences of various women across the generations: to return to my opening theme, these plays, striking as they are, don't add up to an art-form as central to our culture as a fully thriving theatre should be and has been. Is there *any* postwar play with that kind of stature? What of *Waiting for Godot*? In this play of course, we have a different mode: instead of the heightened naturalism of Storey that renders the poetry of ordinary experience and everyday lives, we have an extended metaphor or image, endlessly resonant and suggestive, concentrating experience, subtracting elements from ordinary life yet paradoxically seeming to increase the power, and intimate human relevance, in proportion to the stripping down. Vladimir and Estragon above all are, of course, a couple: their relationship is a habit and a routine (in every sense a comedy routine, a musical hall routine, a Chaplinesque routine); it is a torment and a solace; being together is both an endless tedium and an infinite resource; there are the petty irritations of physicality but, to recall Simone Weil, each is also the destiny of the other. I like to suggest to students that there is something of almost every relationship there: they are friends, they are like siblings (they play at being Lucky and Pozzo), they are like lovers (resolving that it would be better if they parted), they are like parent and child (Vladimir sings a lullaby), and there's almost an 'any wife to any husband' feel at times (they know each other so well, and complete each other's thoughts).

This is a *comic* masterpiece where the comedy is sometimes knock-about, but often rather more rueful, reflecting back to us our feebleness, pretension or self-importance. Pozzo is self-pitying and attention-seeking, and gives his 'artistic performance', his lyrical effusion on the sunset, for which he seeks approval and praise, all while seemingly oblivious to his dehumanizing treatment of Lucky. Vladimir, faced with Lucky and Pozzo lying powerless on the ground calling for help, launches a philosophical disquisition on the need to act when the call for action comes, and drifts on into sheer verbiage, leaving them there. They eventually help Pozzo, but the already victimized 'menial' Lucky is savagely kicked before *he* is helped. The play does not shy away from man's inhumanity to man, but the comedy can also be redemptive, in the sense of drawing us back to a sense of our common humanity: laughter as sharing that and celebrating it even, despite everything. There are moments when everything freezes, and something like acceptance (What is it? Courage? Resilience? Stoicism isn't quite right) is conveyed. Out of talk over food and appetite and attitude this passage emerges:

> *Vladimir*: Question of temperament.
> *Estragon*: Of character.
> *Vladimir*: Nothing you can do about it.
> *Estragon*: No use struggling.
> *Vladimir*: One is what one is.
> *Estragon*: No use wriggling.
> *Vladimir*: The essential doesn't change.
> *Estragon*: Nothing to be done.

After Pozzo's comically dire lyrical effusion on the sunset there is a long silence, and then:

> *Estragon*: So long as one knows.
> *Vladimir*: One can bide one's time.
> *Estragon*: One knows what to expect.
> *Vladimir*: No further need to worry.
> *Estragon*: Simply wait.
> *Vladimir*: We're used to it.

A moment of extraordinary calm.

The play is poetic drama, too, in that it works through the interplay of symbols and images and refrains. There is the lovely moment of the sudden onset of night and the rise of the moon, at the end of Act I, where Estragon stares up at the quaint, comic stage moon, quotes 'Pale for weariness', and places his boots, in a rare (perhaps his only?) moment of unselfishness, where he intends to leave them:

> *Vladimir*: What are you doing with your boots?
>
> *Estragon*: I'm leaving them there. Another will come, just as ... as ... as me, but with smaller feet, and they'll make him happy.

Here, Beckett's exquisite feel for the poetry of dialogue comes out in the hesitation, the catch in the voice. It follows the passage about Estragon's sense of his life as a slow crucifixion, but it appears that someone *does* take the boots; though nothing is certain in this play, and Estragon, who can't be bothered with remembering anything, has forgotten that he put them there. When they do rediscover the boots in Act II, he claims they are not his, as they are a different colour. Someone with smaller feet has exchanged them for his, and left boots which fit when he eventually gets them on! And so we have this small little-noticed moment of mutual helpfulness through exchange-at-a-distance, initiated by the usually completely self-absorbed Estragon.

A little earlier Vladimir shows *some* solicitude for the boy, and establishes some gentle fellow feeling: 'You're not unhappy? Do you hear me?/ Yes, sir./ Well?/ I don't know sir./ You don't know if you're unhappy or not?/ No, sir./ You're like myself.' Such moments are balanced, outweighed, I suppose, by moments of great anguish, such as the terror of emptiness that invades them, or Estragon's great cry for pity, or Pozzo's terrible outburst on the irrelevance of time.

What does one do with this play in the classroom? One trusts it to make its impact, I think: read it right through, taking reactions, clarifying, sharing puzzlement; get students to work out why there are *two* Acts in this seemingly uneventful and repetitive play; and why there aren't three Acts! Once the play is well known, its 'everyman' feel and ambition can be discussed at length: how much experience does the play concentrate? What is missing? It's surprising how far you can get before a student raises the issue of the absence of female characters.

Do we experience claustrophobia in this play? Or is there a sense of grandeur about it? It has its limitations. There is the attitude to bodily existence: disgust. And there is the sense of life as an agony, physically excruciating, a desert of tedium and minor irritation, teased by an endlessly delayed, increasingly improbable 'salvation', barely enough to keep the characters from suicide. There is the 'maleness', perhaps, of the whole perspective of the play. And yet the more I read it and watch it, the more this play seems as close as we get in our time to a play with the powerful centrality of the drama of Shakespeare and the Greeks. I'm not suggesting *as good as*, just the same kind of power and centrality.

Beckett's short plays are also worth exploring. Almost equally powerful, especially in performance, is *Catastrophe*, a play he wrote for Vaclav Havel when the latter was a dissident writer rather than a president. A director and his female assistant work on a figure, an utterly abject, motionless man, on a low black block on the stage, adjusting his pose in small ways, until at the end, having created the image (of catastrophe?) he wants, the director exclaims in pleasure, there is distant muffled applause from somewhere, the play seems to be over, and then the man unexpectedly raises his head, slowly, to stare out at the audience, silencing the applause, and, by implication, *us*. It is brief and very powerful. It has obvious political implications, but it is also an artist's radical self-questioning.

I'll end with a prose-poem-cum-monologue which a student, Lisa Lay, wrote, in role as the motionless figure:

I'm so cold, so utterly, completely, desolately cold. How long am I to stand here? How much longer is this to go on? Surely I've sated his appetite by now. Of how much entertainment can I be? Just to stand here, stripped of all dignity, a pathetic, shivering shell of a man. When will it end? What more does he want? I've complied with his every wish; is that not enough?

So cold! Have lost all feeling in my legs. Still not enough! Yet more to endure! Switch off! Think of something else. Must detach myself from this. Won't let him have my soul, my mind, my life. Must keep control. Don't give in. Must think. Think of what? Something. Anything. Keep my mind focused. Wholesome, pure, unspoiled thoughts. Memories.

A birthday. Aged 6. A smiling, fresh-faced boy waiting, patiently waiting. What for? Father! Wonderful father; friend, confidant, mentor. So long ago; hard to picture him. Try harder. Concentrate! That's it! I see him. He's coming to the door. What's that in his hands? Is it for me? It is. The wooden railway he promised me. He didn't forget.

Picture's fading. Don't go father. Don't go! Stay with me. Gone. Too tired to concentrate; too tired to fight; too tired to care. Do what you will.

Chapter 10

Teaching Literature Post-18
What we read; how we read

Robert Eaglestone

The subject English is the giant of the curriculum devouring the largest share of the timetabled space. Yet, as has often been pointed out, it is the least subject like of subjects, the least susceptible to definition by reference to the accumulation of wisdom with a single academic discipline. No single set of informing ideas dominate its heartland. No one can confidently map its frontiers: it colonizes and is colonized. When we inspect the practices which cluster together uncomfortably under its banner, they appear so diverse, contradictory, arbitrary and random as to defy analysis and explanation.

(Harold Rosen, *Neither Bleak House or Liberty Hall: English in the Curriculum* (London: Institute of Education, 1981), p. 5)

INTRODUCTION

What Harold Rosen said about English in 1981 is still the case: if anything, the subject has become, as Jeremy Paxman might say, even more fissiparous. In part, this is to do with the influx of what's called, reductively, 'literary theory'. The aim of this book has been to look at where text, teacher and student meet. Following this remit the aim of this chapter is twofold: to outline what happens in teaching English post-18 and to see how this reflects back on what secondary level teachers do. Much of the discussion will be involved with 'literary theory', and the similarities and differences between higher and secondary education.

But first, a caveat. English in secondary education and English in higher education are not altogether the same: one is not the 'higher version' of the other. This is much less frequently recognized than you might expect. Not only are there institutional differences, but the ideas taught, the books read and liked or disliked, the behaviour learned from class discussion and many other factors, all mean that English in secondary education is more significant than merely training for a three- or four-year degree in English, literary studies or cultural studies. English in secondary education is not simply a ramp to English in higher education. Moreover, and as this volume shows, despite having common ground with its higher education counterpart, secondary level English contains a range of different aims, methods and objectives. In fact, it would be possible to argue convincingly that the core of the subject 'English' – inasmuch as it has a core – is located in secondary schools, not the universities. After all, in educational terms, the years 11–18 are usually more important than any three-year period post-18.

This said, however, it does seem useful and important to have a clear sense of how the subject connects across the secondary/tertiary divide. This connection is important for the students. After all, according to the most recent UCAS figures I could find (1997), 54,595 students applied to do English in HE, making it the most popular arts and humanities subject, and the seventh most popular subject overall. (The subjects and number of applications in order: Business management 157,253; Law 84,228; Computer science 75,530; Design studies 65,373; Pre-clinical medicine 59,865; Psychology 56,179; English 54,595. The next highest arts and humanities subjects were History 35,866 and Drama 36,085. Figures from the UCAS website www.ucas.ac.uk). Students should know what sort of things English in higher education involves. More ominously, anecdotal evidence from students and from secondary and HE teachers suggests that the jump between secondary and HE level in English is, simply, huge, and significantly wider than for other subjects. I have discussed this at length in my book for A/AS-Level students (*Doing English: A Guide for Literature Students* (London: Routledge, 1999)). I believe that this 'gap' will remain for a considerable time unless and until wider structural and intellectual changes filter through the whole educational system (I suggest some of those intellectual changes at the end of this chapter). In the face of this gap, students should be aware of the differences and similarities in the subject.

But the onus isn't just on the students: a connection is also important for teachers and academics, not least so that both parties can have appropriate expectations of their students. But I also feel that both teachers and academics should have a sense of 'what's going on' both as professionals in education and as specialists at different levels in a wide general field. This is despite – or perhaps because of – the lack of a 'core' to English studies. There is no agreed core to English as a subject and I suspect (and secretly rather hope) that there could not be one. However, the lack of a 'philosophically coherent' core doesn't mean that we can't consider an array of practices and habits under a general label of 'English', and it is to this I now turn.

ENGLISH IN HIGHER EDUCATION (1): A UNIFIED SUBJECT?

In response to the uncertainties in the higher education sector at around the time of the Dearing Report in July 1997, the Council for College and University English (CCUE, or 'see-queue', which I always think sounds much more dramatic) commissioned a report to investigate the contents of the HE English curriculum. Using a large questionnaire sent to all English departments in HE institutions, the report covered not only what was taught, but the principles behind the pedagogical choices made, the amount of cross-institutional consensus or diversity and wider issues arising from debates in and about 'English'. It thus provides the best possible snapshot of English in higher education in terms both of teaching practice and in the curriculum. I will use information from this report, as well as anecdotal evidence, to describe some of the key differences between HE and secondary education. (For more information, see The Council for College and University English, *The English Curriculum: Diversity and Standards: A Report Delivered to the Quality Assurance Agency*, 1997.)

In the first year, most institutions offer a 'foundation course'. This includes studying one or more of the following: 'practical criticism' (87 per cent of institutions); literary theory (79 per cent); how 'literary theory' varies from the next most popular subject, 'key critical concepts' (60 per cent), isn't clear; genres (73 per cent); a literary period (55 per cent) and the English language (51 per cent). Basically, the student will be doing some more abstract work – practical criticism, theory, key concepts – hand-in-hand with the study of particular genres or periods. Thirty-six per cent of institutions also have Old English or medieval courses in this foundation year, and 26 per cent offer creative writing (although how many of these courses would produce anything as good as 'The Wedding Story' that Sue Gregory discusses (pp. 18–19) is open to question). Nearly all claim to provide training in library use and essay-writing skills, usually outside the department in institution-wide programmes. In my experience these are usually rather poorly attended by students. The foundation year is supposed to introduce sophisticated ideas, new concepts and advanced reading skills.

All but two of the respondents claim that the movement from this foundation period to the rest of the degree is part of a structured progression, moving from the general to the more particular. The second and third years have increasing numbers of options, with increasing specialism and a wider range of choice. However, there are still compulsory courses, and these, to me, seem to reflect the practical reality of the day-to-day content of English in HE. The compulsory courses, in order of popularity among departments, are: Shakespeare; Theory; Romantic writing; Renaissance poetry; Victorian fiction; Renaissance drama; Modernist literature; Eighteenth-century literature. This list contrasts with the optional courses the students want to take and are offered by the departments. In order of preference and popularity they are: Women's writing; Shakespeare; Late twentieth-century literature; American writing; Victorian writing; Romantic writing; Modernist writing; Creative writing; Colonial and postcolonial literature; The novel; Gender, sexuality, feminism (why, one might ask, are these grouped together by the survey?); Renaissance writing. This last group might be interpreted to show up an important divide between 'English by period' and 'English by theme'. On the one side are, for example, courses on Romantic and Victorian writing: the 'same old chronological thing'. On the other are courses on, for example, gender, or colonial and postcolonial literature, that have arisen out of 'theoretical' discussions. This is a very rough division (I can imagine a very avant-garde Victorian literature course and a very traditional colonial writing course); however, it does bear the traces of the stresses in the subject – it's no longer just *Beowulf* to Virginia Woolf.

Despite the reputation of English as a very diverse subject, the report claimed to have found 'a remarkable degree of consistency regarding structure, aims and objectives in English, particularly in the concept of a dynamic curriculum which is responsive to student needs and the vigorously developing nature of the subject'. If one were suspicious, this 'consistency' might appear to be less convincing. After all, a responsive, 'dynamic curriculum' just means 'trying to keep the course up to date'. 'Structure' is usually imposed from above on universities. 'Aims and objectives' can often be boiled down to 'education' (or even 'education, education, education', a cause we all think is worthwhile). The presentation of the answers seems prone to offering a more 'unified' vision (e.g. the grouping of 'gender, sexuality, feminism', the 'key critical concepts'). Moreover, this consistency looks questionable in light of what departments thought was important in English (apart, that is, from the key skills taught). Seventy-four per cent of departments thought that a knowledge of the historical, intellectual and cultural context of literature is essential; 72 per cent thought a knowledge of theoretical approaches essential. Only 45 per cent thought that a knowledge of the canon was essential, though 42 per cent thought it desirable. These seem to pick up on quite profound differences. The suspicious person might surmise that the CCUE report was keen to present English as a united front to ... well, to whoever. English, even before its birth as a subject in a recognizable form at around the time of the First World War, has never been without its harsh critics. In a sense, and despite the report's rhetoric, this diversity is no surprise and reflects the 'coreless' nature of English. In the area of actual teaching practice in HE, however, there were more similarities between institutions. It is here, also, that the differences between A/AS-Level and higher education come most clearly into focus.

ENGLISH IN HIGHER EDUCATION (2): TEACHING IN PRACTICE

The CCUE report reveals that almost all HE departments teach through lecture and seminar, although 22 per cent of them offered self-access and/or distance learning. Nine per cent have student-led workshops. In HE, the average contact time is eight hours per week, presumably mostly with different staff. This means that the learning experience is very different – much more 'self-directed'. Anecdotally, one of the most common problems which first-year students have is precisely this shift from the more directed secondary learning to the more self-directed HE style. Rather ironically, it seems to me, the better the secondary teaching, the worse, often, this jump for the student. The inspiring A/AS-Level teacher has two years to encourage exploration and intellectual ambition, often with several contact hours per week. The individual HE lecturer, however inspiring, has only a few weeks to achieve the same effect, usually in a large lecture. This often makes the student feel that no one is interested in her or his progress, which can, understandably, put off some students.

Another difference in teaching practice which students find very stressful, again anecdotally, is in the number of texts they have to read and ideas they have to cover. According to the QCA guidelines, at A/AS-Level, students study in detail a minimum of eight texts covering prose, poetry and drama (including a play by Shakespeare, at least two texts published before 1900 and at least one work published before 1770). Although many schools do more than this over the two years, it is not unusual to expect HE students to cover this in *two weeks*. (Imagine, for the sake of illustration, four courses a term: 'Shakespeare'; 'The novel 1700–1900'; 'Romantic poetry'; 'Women's writing'. This week: *Macbeth*, half of *Tom Jones*, *Lyrical Ballads* and Jean Rhys's *Wide Sargasso Sea*. Next week: *Hamlet*, the other half of *Tom Jones*, Books I and II of *The Prelude*, Toni Morison's *Sula*. All this while working on an essay on the role of authority in Shakespeare's Roman plays.) That said, and assuming a thirty-five hour working week (!), this is twenty-seven hours of reading and research time after lectures and seminars, obviously much more than one could do while taking two to four other subjects at A/AS-Level. And, as I remind students, their ability to process information gets quicker and quicker.

However, one of the major factors in the 'jump' from secondary to HE is the dramatic increase in importance given to theory in HE: as I have noted, 72 per cent of departments thought a knowledge of theoretical approaches essential. To write very frankly, from my experience and that of other academics, A/AS-Level has been to date, in the majority of cases, poor preparation for grasping the ideas and wider issues that the study of literary theory raises. Of course, there are exceptions and exceptional teachers, and this book contains some of them. But, in general, and not to put too fine a point on it, A/AS-Level English does not teach students – or even prepare them – to think about hard literary issues. In addition, when asked to think about these issues, many of them, used to processing opinions and facts without thinking them through or weighing them up, find it hard or impossible. This leads to a great deal of dissatisfaction on their part ('this isn't what I came to do': 'it makes me feel so stupid') and on the part of academics ('what can't they understand?').

I have stated this very strongly, so let me qualify this claim to some extent. By 'theory', I simply mean a catch-all term for a huge range of new and different ways of reading and interpreting texts that have so influenced English in HE in the last twenty years or so. I do not refer to any particular theoretical approach (deconstructive, new historicist, cultural materialist, etc.). I would argue that most so-called 'theoretical' ideas emerge fairly easily from discussions of texts – think about the wide-ranging discussions in your very best lessons and seminars, which broaden out from the particular text to other, very real issues in your and your students' lives, and in the world. This is 'theory', if unsystematized (the best way, perhaps?). A colleague of mine, Jennifer Bavidge, argues that all 17-year-olds are 'natural theorists', as their intellectual range and ambition is not grounded only in the text itself but in an attempt to integrate the texts they study with their life and wider concerns in general. (This urge to integrate texts and life seems to be reflected in the success of the 'teen-lit' movies, which show teenagers' lives shaped by classic texts, for example, *Clueless/Emma* or *10 Things I Hate about You/The Taming of the Shrew*. These are not just retellings of 'the story' but are about exactly this integration, about the way literature can give shape to life.)

By 'teaching theory', I also don't mean to sound like those academics (more caricatured than real, I suspect) who despair because their first-year English students can't understand an advanced discussion by

Derrida of an obscure footnote in Hegel. To expect this is not only counter-productive, it is also rather arrogant and just plain silly – after all, just as physics students work up to advanced understandings of quantum states, so English students work up to more advanced ideas. Nor do I believe that the teaching of literature should be given over to just the teaching of, say, Michel Foucault and Donna Harraway (although I teach these two, among other philosophers and theorists, with great pleasure). However, as a 'theory teacher', it does make me a little annoyed to discover that hardly any first-year English students have any idea at all about, for example, debates over authorial intention: after all, this discussion has been going on for over *fifty years* in English. Again, students seem to know nothing about, for example, feminist approaches to literature, despite offering rather good – if informal – feminist critiques of, say, *Ally McBeal*. Worst of all – very much worst of all – most first-year students seem to have no idea that there might be more than one interpretation of any particular text. This is particularly irritating because actually they know, from their own life experience (for example, watching *Ally McBeal* and arguing about it with their friends), that there is more than one interpretation of any text. That they think there isn't is because of what Patrick Scott calls, in his excellent book *Reconstructing 'A' level English*, the 'common heritage of teaching about literature'. This heritage, he argues, is 'actively disabling' (see Patrick Scott, *Reconstructing 'A' level English* (Buckingham: Open University Press, 1989), p. 19ff.). I have discussed this at length and in detail – and clearly enough, I hope, for students to read – in *Doing English*. Some of the feedback on this book, received between submitting this chapter and revising it for publication, suggests that a larger number of teachers than I thought (a significant minority, as it were) are rejecting this 'disabling heritage' and putting these 'theoretical' ideas into action. There are changes afoot in the A/AS-Level curriculum and more secondary level teachers are coming through the system who have studied the broader issues about literature that 'theory' raises. The new Qualifications and Curriculum Authority guidelines and new syllabi, treading carefully between the 'traditionalist' and 'theoretical' camps, offer room for more stimulating and innovative approaches which will, in turn, make students more able to cope with English in higher education. This makes me feel very optimistic, but these changes are still in their early stages, and the result of work by a significant minority.

ACROSS THE GAP

What does all this mean for the teaching of English 11–18? As I have suggested above, the lack of 'theory' at A/AS-Level causes a huge gap between English 11–18 and English post-18. (This is a terrible over-simplification: in fact, English is much more complex and mosaic-like than this.) Two arguments follow from this for teaching literature 11–18. One rather coercive argument might state that, as the clock can't be turned back and the subject has changed so much at HE, teaching literature 11–18 must change too (although, as my introductory caveat suggested, this doesn't necessarily follow). However, less aggressively, I would argue that teaching English more 'theoretically' makes the subject more relevant, more important in people's lives and – if you will excuse the grandiose nature of the claim, unsupported here – more ethical. (I argue this claim in detail in *Ethical Criticism* (Edinburgh: Edinburgh University Press, 1997).) Of course, many teachers (for example, in this volume) are already teaching in a more 'theory-influenced' way. The new QCA guidelines can be interpreted as more 'theoretical', too. However, from the point of view of a teacher in higher education, I want to outline three ideas that I would like to see made clear for secondary level English teaching. These are not a 'core' for the subject and certainly not a 'new way' of doing English. Instead, they are points for orientation.

First, English deals with texts, certainly, but not just with what we read. It also explores *how we read*. It is about the interpretation of texts and ideas that arise from interpretation. Montaigne wrote that 'we need to interpret interpretations more than we interpret things': how we interpret texts is absolutely central to the world today. Moreover, exploring how we read is also 'learning about learning' and so adds to a wider range of skills and ideas that will continually develop through a student's life. This picks up – and perhaps expands – the QCA's assessment objectives:

> 2.2 ... AS courses should encourage candidates to reflect on their own responses to texts, considering other readers' interpretations; 3.2 ... candidates to show knowledge and understanding of ... the different ways in which texts are interpreted by different readers, acknowledging that literary texts have a range of meanings and the significance of these is related to readers' knowledge, experience and ideas; 3.3 ... the ways in which texts have been interpreted and valued by different readers at different times, acknowledging that interpretation of literary texts can depend on a reader's assumptions and stance.

There are a number of ramifications to this. One is, of course, the need to jettison once and for all the already crumbling myth of 'objectivity' in English. Put simply, there is no right answer. This means, in turn, thinking through the nature and scope of assessment. It also means opening up English to a radical pluralism, where many ways of doing English are considered to be valid. A traditional Leavisite way of approaching literature should be given room, as well as theoretical approaches, whether 'home grown' or imported from the USA or Paris. The difference is that all ways of doing English should be up front about the presuppositions they are making. This also means that we should avoid simply replacing 'one way of doing English' with 'another way of doing English'. This is a problem for the 'Critical Literacy' movement: though admirable in many ways, it does want to replace an 'old way' of doing English with a single 'new way'. (For examples of this see Wendy Morgan, *Critical Literacy in the Classroom* (London: Routledge, 1997) and Chris Searle's rather inspiring *None but Our Words: Critical Literacy in the Classroom and Community* (Buckingham: Open University Press, 1998).) English, as Harold Rosen pointed out nearly twenty years ago, is an open-ended pluralist subject, which accepts a wide range of approaches.

Second, because of its development and content, English is a very diffuse subject. In one sense it is an 'under-labourer' to other disciplines, not just because it teaches skills of literacy, writing and reflection, but because it examines interpretation, which is vital for other subjects on the curriculum. But English is also a subject where a huge range of ideas are played with, constructed, taken apart, argued over and so on. It reflects the infinite scope that literature displays, and should perhaps demonstrate this flexibility more frequently. A consequence of this 'diffuseness' is the endless controversy that surrounds English. Because the subject has no one obvious core, everyone with an agenda wants to claim that the particular issues which concern them are central to English. Another consequence is the 'pluralism' discussed above. This diffuseness and openness seem to me to be more a cause of celebration than worry.

Third, English, as culture and as a subject which studies culture, is involved with our relationships with others and with the world. Culture is woven inextricably into politics, understood at its most basic as 'how we get along', and has far-reaching effects in the wider world. A consequence of this is that English is not just about texts, but also about each of us, about others and about the nature of society. This is absolutely not to take a Marxist line over English which would claim that English is a site for activism and cultural politics, although such a position is, in some ways, admirable. It is rather to say only that English as a subject is culturally and politically important. As Brian Cox argued, specifically over the National Curriculum, 'control of the National Curriculum can lead to control of the way children think. A national curriculum in English influences attitudes to class and race' (Brian Cox,

Cox on the Battle for the English Curriculum (London: Hodder & Stoughton, 1995), p. 23).

These three suggestions aim to lead English to question its presuppositions more clearly. They are all fairly straightforward and have already been implemented in many schools and colleges and can be seen, I would suggest, in the new QCA guidelines. A benefit of foregrounding these 'orientations' would be to reduce considerably the gap between secondary and higher English education.

CONCLUSION

One of the saddest things I read in relation to teaching English was this comment by an English teacher about teaching Shakespeare:

> when kids go 'I hate Shakespeare' I can honestly say 'I really understand that, I'm not telling you that it's brilliant'. And sometimes they ask 'Why have we got to study this?' and the personal side of me thinks 'I haven't got an answer for that – I had to, you have to' . . . it's never very satisfactory.
>
> (John Yandell, 'Reading Shakespeare, or Ways with Will',
> in *Changing English*, 4: 2 (1997), p. 278)

The worst thing I can think of in the study of literature is for it to become a bland heritage ritual studying a desiccated library of texts: 'I had to, you have to.' 'Do it because it's always been done' is, in itself, no argument for anything. Theory, at all levels, is a way of avoiding this. Thinking and teaching about *how we read and interpret* – doing 'theory' – makes literature more open and more clearly part of people's lives, more clearly part of education.

Index